A Thread Runs Through It

THE QUILTS,
THE STORIES,
THE STEPS

BARBARA DIEGES

American
Quilter's
Society

P.O. Box 3290 • Paducah, KY 42002-3290
www.AQSquilt.com

Located in Paducah, Kentucky, the American Quilter's Society (AQS) is dedicated to promoting the accomplishments of today's quilters. Through its publications and events, AQS strives to honor today's quiltmakers and their work and to inspire future creativity and innovation in quiltmaking.

Editor: Marjorie L. Russell
Graphic Design: Lisa M. Clark
Cover Design: Michael Buckingham
Photography: Charles R. Lynch
    Vintage photographs provided by the author

Library of Congress Cataloging-in-Publication Data
Dieges, Barbara
    A thread runs through it : the quilts, the stories, the steps / by Barbara Dieges.
       p. cm.
       ISBN 1-57432-793-3
    1. Patchwork--Patterns. 2. Appliqué--Patterns. 3. Quilting. I. Title.
       TT835 .D524 2002
       746.46'041--dc21
                              2002009669

Additional copies of this book may be ordered from the American Quilter's Society,
PO Box 3290, Paducah, KY 42002-3290, or online at www.AQSquilt.com.

ACKNOWLEDGMENTS

As this book comes to fruition, my heartfelt thanks goes to my quilting friends
Sonny Buhrer
Ann Dante
Terisa Edwards
Grace Hoya
Patti Lantz
Marji Martin
Diane Mattern
Sally Potter
Marge Sheppard
Bonnie Ussery
who helped me read through
all the material.

Thanks also to Sally Fimbres who appliquéd the roses on MY WILD ROSE and Betty Steen who entrusted me with her antique quilt.

I *appreciate* that Sandra Kuehn, Dolores Tversky, Ann Webster, Susan B. Tully M.D., Patty Wootton, Michi Murayama, and Nancy Hogue were there with gentle prodding, encouragement, and friendship.

I AM INDEBTED

...to my *mother*, Mary Seiler, who sewed many quilt bindings and whose life experiences were the inspiration for some of the stories in this book;

...to my *children* – Jennifer, Eric, and Laura – who love my quilts and whose stories are also included here, and;

...to my *husband*, Tom. I could not have accomplished what I have without his encouragement. He gave me many hugs when I felt discouraged, and he believed in me. This faith was the connecting thread that stitched the stories and quilts together.

CONTENTS

Let's take a step back in time to a time when life was slower. In that era, the people made do or did without. They took joy in simple pleasures. Even though life was hard, the spirit of community brought them together. During those hard times, the sincere spirits of the people and their concern for others served them well.

Meet Anna Maria Saller who was born in 1839 on a small farm in the eastern United States. Her parents were immigrants from Bavaria. Anna married John Ellison, a joiner or cabinet maker, in 1866. For a time they lived with her family on the farm.

When their children were small, John and Anna made the decision to return to his home in the small mountain community of Thistle Hollow, where he had inherited some land.

These are their stories.

Anna remembers...

Supplies

The items listed here will be used in the making of some or all of the quilts. See the author's personal preferences for many of these supplies in the Resources section (pg. 110).

100% cotton fabric in prints, plaids, and solids

Sewing machine with a ¼" seam allowance foot

Needles
Jeans/Denim 80/12 sewing machine needles or
    Quilting Needles 75/11 – 90/12
#12 Betweens for hand quilting
#12 Betweens or sharps for appliqué

Thread
Silk Finish 100% Cotton Thread
    Size 50 for hand appliqué, machine
    sewn patches, and machine quilting
100% Cotton quilting thread
    Size 40 for hand quilting

Rulers and markers
Rulers 6" x 24", 6" x 6", and 6" x 12"
Quarter-inch marker (a)
Angle and corner marker (b)
.05 mechanical pencil
.05B lead for mechanical pencil
White and silver pencils
Slivers of white hand soap

Cutting tools
Rotary cutter in any size
Rotary cutting mat
Small scissors and snips for cutting threads
Large scissors for cutting fabric
Large scissors for cutting plastic and paper

Other useful tools and supplies
Fine straight pins .05
Thimble
Finger protector
Used rubber glove (cut off the fingers)
Blue painter's masking tape (does not leave residue)
100% cotton needle punched batting
Small calculator
Liquid or spray starch
Heat resistant template plastic
Freezer paper – plastic coated paper commonly
    available in the paper goods aisle of grocery stores

Why is it that some men will buy something for you without even asking if you have need of it?

Now I'd been doing right fine piecing my quilts by hand, making the best stitches I could. Sure, I didn't get as many done as I'd like, but I kept us in warm covers.

Well, John came home from the city one day, and he drove straight to the barn. That seemed mighty odd, as he usually stopped at the house first.

When he came in the house, he looked serious. He said, "You've got to come up to the barn. It's important." I thought, now what?

When I saw the barn door closed, I thought, "Oh my, the cow's died and he's breaking it to me gentle." But she'd been fine that morning when I milked her. John opened the barn door, and there on the wagon was something covered with a blanket. He jumped up on the wagon and whipped off the blanket.

Beneath was some kind of contraption made of metal and wood. "Now what is that," I wondered! "What's so special about this? What am I supposed to think?"

Finally, he said proudly, "There was a man in the city and he was showing just how much time this could save for our wives. So I thought you could use it."

I said, "Well, what is it and how can I use it if I don't know what it is?"

Then he explained that it was a sewing machine. I just looked at him and shook my head.

When we finally got it into the house, John showed me how to push the pedal to make the needle go up and down. It took me a while, but I got the hang of it, though that first time I shouldn't have spent so much time at it, because my legs did ache!

When I became comfortable with it, my piecing did fly through that machine. I even did some piecing for my neighbors till they got their own sewing machines.

First I had the sewing machine against the wall, but my back was to everything, so I turned it around so I could see what was going on.

Now if John had asked me first, I would have told him I had no need of something like that. But then, all those quilts would never have been made!

So maybe that's why they don't ask us first.

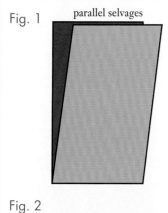

Fig. 1
parallel selvages

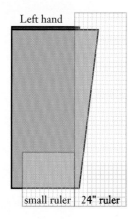

Fig. 2

Right hand

24" ruler | small ruler

Left hand

small ruler | 24" ruler

If you are right-handed, place the edge to be cut off toward the left. If you are left-handed, place the edge to be cut off toward the right.

Fig. 3

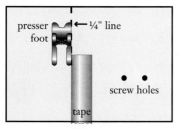

presser foot

← ¼" line

screw holes

tape

BASIC INFORMATION

Whatever quilt you choose to make, there are several things to consider. Here are the basics:

Pre-washing

Depending on the quilt, I may or may not pre-wash fabrics before using them. If an antique look is desired, I often don't pre-wash the fabrics. Instead I do it after the quilt is quilted, finished, and bound. Waiting until the end shrinks the fabrics and draws the quilt up slightly, giving it a more uneven look. Colors slightly blending into each other also contributes to an older look.

However, to prevent excessive bleeding, especially with dark fabrics, you may want to pre-wash fabrics with a dye stabilizer. If you wash some of the fabrics in the quilt, you should wash all of them, including the backing. Of course, always wash light fabrics separately from dark ones.

Fabric strip cutting

The strip piecing calculations for the patterns in this book are based on 42" wide fabric. Although most quilting fabric is labeled 44" or 45" wide, the amount a fabric shrinks during pre-washing and the size of the selvages (finished edges) can substantially reduce the useable width. Unless stated otherwise, strips are cut across the width of the fabric, from selvage to selvage.

(Fig. 1) Bring the selvages together with wrong sides facing. The fabric should lie flat. The cut edges may not align, but it is important that the selvages line up without pleats, folds, or wrinkles in the fabric.

(Fig. 2) Place a line on a small ruler along the fold and position a 24" ruler against it, covering the ragged edge. Once the large ruler is positioned, remove the small ruler. To make the first cut, hold the 24" ruler firmly, "walking" your hand up the ruler, parallel to the cutter. Proceed in the same way to cut the strips.

Stitching

Sew all seams with 13–15 stitches per inch. On some machines this is indicated by a numeral but on others, the number of stitches per inch is less obvious.

All of the piecing in this book (and for most quilters everywhere) is based on using a scant ¼" seam allowance. An exact ¼" is too much. The thread and the folds of the patches after being pressed to one side take up space in the seam allowance. Sew a hair's width narrower than a ¼" seam allowance.

(Fig. 3) Mark the edge parallel to your sewing machine needle with tape or a permanent pen mark, or mark in front of the foot for guiding the fabric. If there are screw holes on the bed of the machine, you should be able to use a seam guide attachment for your machine.

Barbara Dieges

Pressing

Press all sewn strips and patches from the front (right side) of the fabric. By pressing from the front, you are less likely to press pleats into the seam lines.

(Fig. 4) If the seam allowance is to be pressed under the darkest fabric, then the darkest fabric should be on top. Pressing the sewn patch sets the seam. Lift the uppermost fabric. With the edge of the iron, press slowly and gently against the seam line. This will flip the piece to the left, or to the right for left-handers. Press the iron down on the patches for a few seconds. Do not move the iron back and forth.

When pressing strips, press the whole sewn strip to set the seam. Then lift the upper fabric and press the length of the iron against the seam line. Repeat along the length of the seam.

Thread saver

A thread saver keeps the back of your work neat and keeps the needle from pushing the beginning of seams into the feed dogs.

(Fig. 5) To make a thread saver, take a scrap of fabric approximately 1" square and fold it in half.

(Fig. 6) Before starting to sew a seam, sew across this small piece of fabric first, making one or two empty stitches between the thread saver and fabric.

(Fig. 7) To end the seam, clip the thread saver off the beginning, sew the seam, position the thread saver in front of the needle, take one or two empty stitches between the fabric and thread saver, then sew across the scrap.

Leave the scrap under the foot and clip off the sewn piece. The thread saver remains under the foot of the machine, ready to start a new seam. When the thread saver is thick with stitches, simply discard it and start again with a new scrap.

APPLIQUÉ

Hints about needles and thread

When preparing to appliqué, match the thread as closely as possible to the motif fabric. If it is a print fabric, choose the predominant color. At times you may need to change colors to match the changing colors in the motif fabric, especially with a large print.

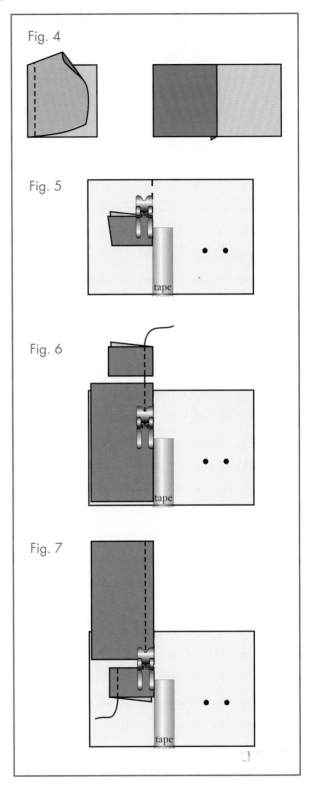

Fig. 4

Fig. 5

tape

Fig. 6

tape

Fig. 7

tape

GENERAL PATCHWORK INSTRUCTIONS

For hand appliqué, unroll the thread from the spool rather than pulling it off the end. Roll the thread back onto the spool after cutting. Use a short (12"–15") single thread for appliqué. Longer threads tend to tangle and fray.

Use a fine needle, a #12 between or sharp is my preference. Dampen the end of the thread and cut through the damp end at a slight angle with sharp scissors. Thread the needle, making the knot at the end cut from the spool.

As you stitch, pull up firmly to set the stitch. The stitch should almost disappear into the fabric. Do not pull too firmly or the fabric will pucker. To end the thread on the wrong side of your work, take several (4–5) small backstitches in different directions and then clip the tail of the thread.

APPLIQUÉ (OR HIDDEN) STITCH: Pin or thread baste the motifs in place on your background fabric. If you prefer to use pins, safety pins are recommended so you won't stick yourself as you sew. Use 1" pins to hold the motifs in place. Use two or more pins depending on the size of the motif.

(Fig. 8) Bring the needle through the back of the base fabric and through the fold of the motif. Pull the thread through. Place the point of the needle below the place where the thread comes out and slightly under the edge of the fold.

Stitch no more than ⅛" into the base fabric. Come back up through the edge of the fold with the point of the needle. This is accomplished with a slight up and down rocking motion of the hand. Pull the thread through until it is taut. Pull enough so the stitch is buried in the fold, but not enough to pucker the motif or background fabric. This is the first stitch.

(Fig. 9) Do not start stitching at a point or a "V." Instead, start in an area that is as straight as possible. Allow for an opening of about ¾" so the paper can be removed later.

(Fig. 10) At an indentation or "V," take two extra deep stitches. There is no seam allowance at this point, and the stitches are the only thing holding this area in place. These stitches will show, so it is important to use matching thread.

(Fig. 11) When there are layers of appliqué motifs, first stitch those pieces that will be underneath other pieces. Stop stitching where edges will be covered by another motif.

(Fig. 12) At a point, take an extra tiny stitch through the last stitch. This extra stitch stabilizes the point. Trim if there is more than ⅛" of fabric showing.

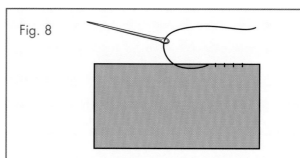

Fig. 8

NOTE: The stitches are shown in Figure 8 to indicate that they are at a 90˚ angle to the edge of the fabric. In reality, the stitches should not show along the folded edge of the motif. On the back side of the base fabric the stitches will be at a slight angle parallel to the edge of the motif.

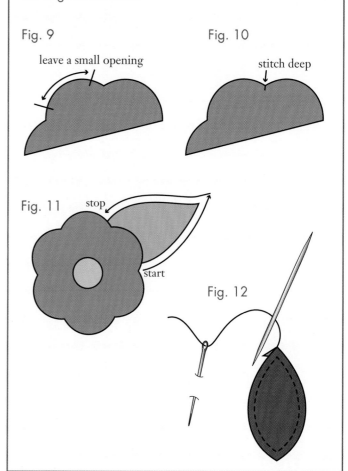

Fig. 9

leave a small opening

Fig. 10

stitch deep

Fig. 11

stop

start

Fig. 12

Barbara Dieges

"Park" the needle. Hold the thread firmly and with the side of a dampened toothpick or heavy pin, sweep the excess seam allowance under the motif. It is not recommended that the side of your needle be used for this purpose since the needle's fine point can shred the tiny seam allowance.

To leave an opening to remove the paper, stop stitching a short distance from the beginning stitches. Park the needle; do not end the stitching or cut the thread.

Freezer paper appliqué

Freezer paper is usually available in the same supermarket aisles as plastic wrap and aluminum foil. The paper has a thin plastic backing that becomes sticky when ironed and adheres to the fabric. Cutting motifs from freezer paper and ironing them to the fabric gives support to the fabric and creates a tiny edge, making it easier to appliqué.

(Fig. 13) Trace motifs onto the dull side of the freezer paper. If the motif is a directional design (such as a letter), reverse it so it is backwards before tracing. For repeat motifs, you can fold the paper and cut up to eight layers at once, depending on the sharpness of your scissors. Trace one motif on the top layer then staple the layers together inside the motif. Cut all layers at once.

(Fig. 14) If the motif is directional, cut the paper roughly to the desired size and stack the pieces paper side up, then staple.

Iron the slick side of the freezer paper to the wrong side of the fabric. The edge of the freezer paper is where the stitching line will be, so remember to leave enough space (at least ½") between the motifs to allow adequate seam allowances around each piece.

(Fig. 15) Add a ¼" seam allowance around the edge of the paper when cutting the fabric. Hold the motif with the paper face up. Snip indentations or inner points ("Vs") in the fabric to the edge of the paper. Turn the seam allowance over the edge of the paper and baste.

Smooth the fabric over the edge of the paper along curves to avoid little bumps. Use the point of your needle or a fingernail to pull the fabric over the edge of the paper to smooth out bumps.

(Fig. 16) When basting curves, you can also use a running stitch in the seam allowance, halfway between the edge of the paper and the edge of the fabric. Start basting at a straight point and then move out to the curve, come back to the paper, and pull up on the thread. This will gather the seam allowance over the edge of the paper.

NOTE: If the point is lumpy, it means there is too much seam allowance beneath. Pick out the stitches and trim back the seam allowance slightly – it may not need much. Finish the stitching.

Fig. 13

The letter E reversed

Fig. 14

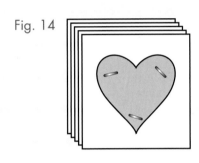

Fig. 15

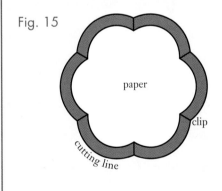

paper

clip

cutting line

Fig. 16

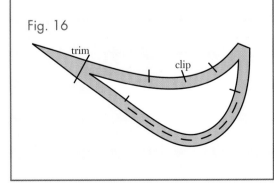

trim

clip

Inner curves or concave edges need to be clipped so the fabric will lay smoothly over the paper. Do not clip all the way to the edge of the paper. Make several clips along the edge of the fabric.

If there are long unwieldy points in pieces like narrow leaves, trim the end of the piece ⅛" from the point of the paper. Trim the seam allowance, leaving ⅛" seam allowance about 1" from the point on both sides (Fig. 16). Do not baste edges that will be covered with another motif.

(Fig. 17) At an inner point where there is no fabric at the bottom of a "V," just baste through the paper and continue.

(Fig. 18) At the point of a motif, continue basting the seam allowance to the edge of the fabric, then stop with the thread on the fabric side.

(Fig. 19) Fold the seam allowance over, bring the needle through the seam allowance, and continue basting down the other side. There will be some fabric sticking out to the side of the point; that is how it should look. It will be taken care of as it is stitched.

REMOVING PAPER: Remove the basting thread and slip tweezers or a hemostat between the paper and motif fabric. The seam allowance will slip out of place.

Move the tool around gently, but don't pierce the fabric. Slide the tool along the edges. If the paper is difficult to remove or sticks to the fabric too tightly, briefly heat the piece with an iron.

(Fig. 20) Grab the paper with the tool and slip the paper out. If the opening is small, give the tool a twist. Hold the tool closed as you pull out the paper. If the paper tears and some is left behind, reach in and grab the remaining paper with the tool. Push the seam allowance back in place and finish the seam.

Needleturn appliqué

This type of appliqué is done without benefit of paper or pre-basting the edges. It is so named because the edges are turned under to a marked line with the side of the needle.

MARKING: The markings must be on the right side of the fabric, so always use a .05 pencil with soft lead or a water soluble pen. On dark fabrics mark with a white or silver pencil (available from quilt shops) or a white china marker (available at stationery stores). Sharpen the tip with an eyebrow pencil sharpener. Turn the marked line under so it will not show.

BASTING AND STITCHING: Thread baste the motif to the base fabric ¼" inside the markings. If the motif is large, it is also good to baste across the center in both directions. Make sure that the motif fabric lies flat against the background. If it is well basted, it becomes one with the background fabric.

Use an appliqué stitch (see page 10) to attach the piece. Do not start stitching at a point or indentation. Bring your needle up through the fold. The seam allowance is turned under as you stitch, swept under the motif with the side of the needle or with a dampened toothpick. Points and "Vs" are treated just as they are in the freezer paper technique.

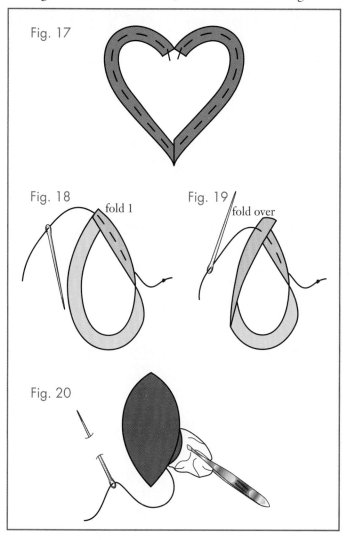

Fig. 17

Fig. 18 fold 1

Fig. 19 fold over

Fig. 20

Vines and stems

Curved vines and stems must be made from bias strips. Bias isn't needed for straight stems.

(Fig. 21) Fold up one corner of the fabric so the raw edge is parallel or even with the selvage.

(Fig. 22) Fold the bias fold over on itself, bringing point A to point B. Trim off the narrowest possible amount from the bias fold. Cut strips to the required width, aligning the ruler with the new cut.

VINE OR STEM #1: This type of vine or stem is useful when you need to cut a large amount for a border or a whole quilt from the same fabric. This stem will be a constant size throughout the project. Probably the narrowest stem you can make will finish to about ³⁄₁₆".

Cut bias strips from the width of the fabric. Fabric that is 42" wide should yield strips about 60" long. Cut strips four times your desired finished width. (For example: ¼" finished x 4 = 1" cut bias strip.) It may not be necessary to join the strips, especially if you need only short pieces or if the ends will be tucked under leaves, flowers, and other stems. If necessary, join the strips as you would join binding strips (pg. 25).

With wrong sides together, fold the bias strip in half lengthwise with raw edges aligned. Press the fold with an iron but do not stretch the strip while pressing.

(Fig. 23) With your sewing machine, stitch slightly less than ¼" from the raw edges, through both layers. Use small stitches, between 12–15 per inch.

Perfect points

Do not miter. Trim straight across the point, leaving a ⅛" seam allowance from the point or line. Trim the edges of the point, leaving a ⅛" seam allowance on both sides of the point.

The seam allowance is turned under as you stitch. At the point take an extra tiny stitch to stabilize it.

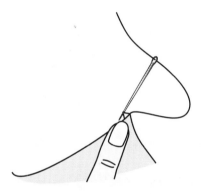

With the side of a heavy pin or a damp toothpick, sweep the seam allowance under the point of the motif and continue stitching.

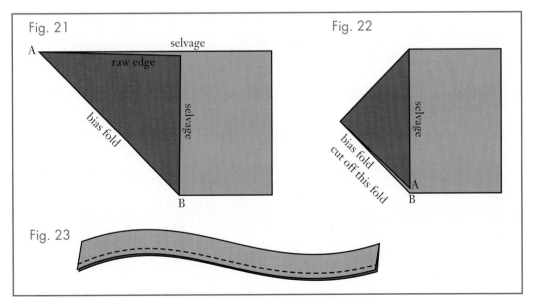

Fig. 21   Fig. 22

Fig. 23

When marking the base fabric for positioning a vine or stem, mark where only one edge of the piece will be placed. It can be difficult to be exact when marking curved parallel lines. Since the bias strip is a uniform width, there's no need for a second mark. You'll also find it easier to cover one line with the fabric so the markings won't show.

Lay the fold of the bias along the line and appliqué the fold to the base fabric. When one side is completely appliquéd, turn under the raw edge so the machine stitch is hidden. Appliqué the second edge.

VINE OR STEM #2: This vine can be made very narrow, slightly less than ⅛". Cut a wider strip than needed because it is easier to handle a wide piece of fabric and trim it, than a narrow piece. Making vines or stems by this technique also allows you to adjust the width of the piece, making portions wider or narrower if you wish.

Cut a 1" strip of bias fabric. Fold it in half with *wrong* sides together and press the fold. Do not stretch or distort the strip while pressing.

(Fig 24) Align the fold along the marked line. Appliqué this fold to the base fabric.

(Fig. 25) Fold the top layer of the vine back and trim the lower seam allowance to less than ⅛".

Trim the top layer to ¼". Cover the ⅛" seam allowance with the top layer. Fold under the raw edge of the top layer and appliqué. To make the seam narrower, you may need to trim away more of the top piece.

Circles

Circles can be made over a foundation or simply gathered into a small "puff," then flattened and appliquéd. Follow the steps for freezer paper motifs, except cut the circle from paper the weight of an index card or file folder. If you prefer, you could also use a heat resistant template plastic.

(Fig. 26) Cut the fabric at least ½" larger than the circle pattern to allow for a ¼" seam allowance all the way around.

> NOTE: The seam allowance beneath the finished circle pads it, making it appear as if it were stuffed. Make your seam allowance slightly larger if you want the circle to be more prominent. The sizes of the circles needed are stated in each pattern.

(Fig. 27) Knot your thread and insert the needle through the right side of the fabric. Make gathering stitches around the edge of the fabric circle.

(Fig. 28) Take one stitch past the knot without catching it, and end on the right side. Pull up the thread to gather the fabric.

Spray the gathers with spray starch, or dip a cotton swab in liquid starch and dampen the gathers. Press firmly with an iron. Pull out the thread by the knot and remove the circle template. The gathers will bounce back and hold quite firmly. The starch can make it difficult to pull the thread. In that case, clip the thread in several places, then spread the gathers to remove the template.

Appliqué in place. This should make a perfect circle without any small points at the edges.

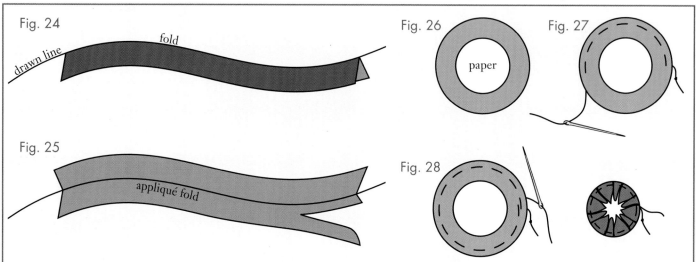

Fig. 24
drawn line   fold

Fig. 25
appliqué fold

Fig. 26
paper

Fig. 27

Fig. 28

DIAMONDS, PARALLELOGRAMS, AND Y-SEAMS

Cutting diamonds from strips

Cutting diamonds from strips is easy. Simply cut a strip of fabric as indicated in the instructions for your quilt.

(Fig. 29) All sides are equal in true diamond patches. The diagonal (45°) measurement of 1b is the same as 1a.

(Fig. 30) Lay the ruler across the strip at a 45° diagonal (1b). Trim off the end of the strip diagonally at a 45° angle.

(Fig. 31) Realign the ruler with the first cut, measure off the amount of 1b, and make the second cut.

(Fig. 32) Repeat to cut the number needed.

Cutting parallelograms from strips

(Fig. 33) Use the same steps to cut parallelograms as diamonds. From a strip of fabric, cut as directed in your quilt instructions, trim off the end of the strip diagonally at a 45° angle. Then measure across the strip the width of the 1b measurement and cut. Repeat to cut the number needed.

(Fig. 34) To make parallelograms or diamonds that are mirror images of each other, cut from doubled fabric or two fabrics layered with right sides together (see below).

Diamonds and parallelograms can also be cut from layered strips that have been sewn with a ¼" seam along one edge. This method means you will handle fewer individual pieces. Make sure your machine is set for a slightly smaller than usual stitch. Since the beginning stitches in each unit will not be anchored with a backstitch, small stitches make the seam less likely to pull open.

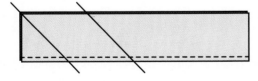

Cut and mark the diamonds, then unpick the seam from the edge of the diamond to the marked point (arrow), at the wide angle but not at the point. To help deter the seam from opening, do not clip the threads you've unpicked. The disadvantage to this method is that the unpicked seam is a weak point in the block since the seam would usually have a backstitch at that point. Proceed with the remaining steps for setting in the triangle or square.

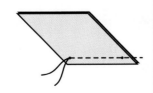

Fig. 29

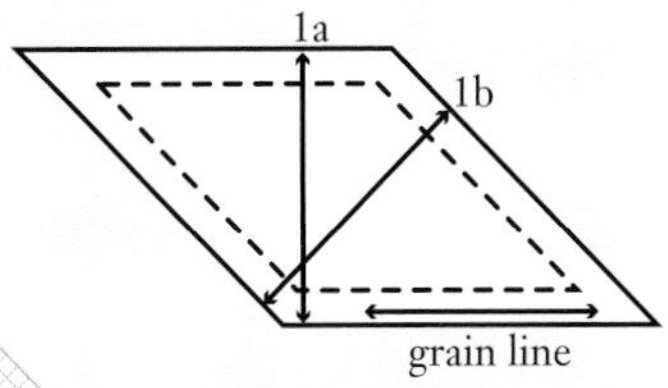

Fig. 30 45°

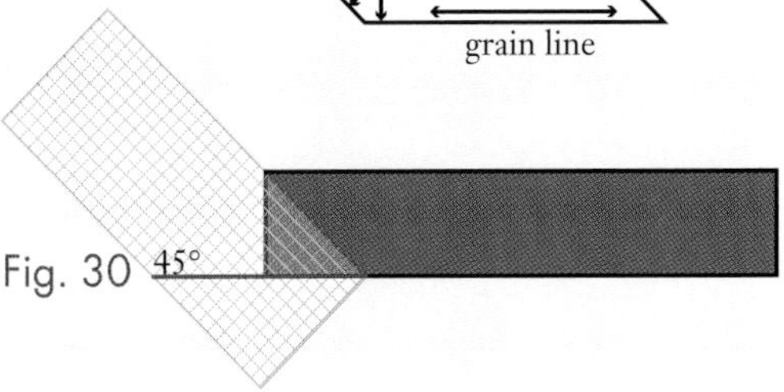

Fig. 31 45°

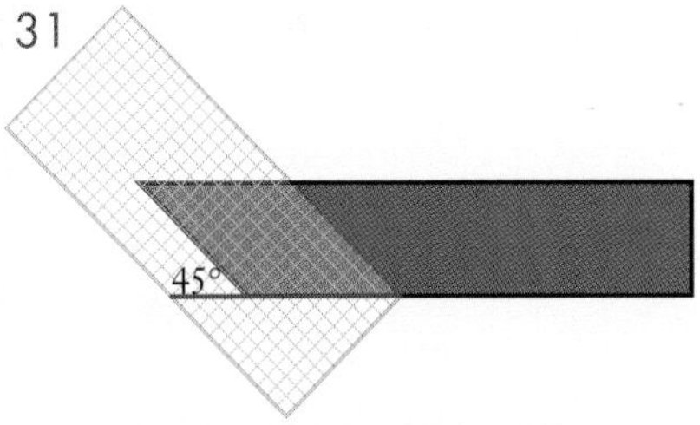

Fig. 32

Fig. 33

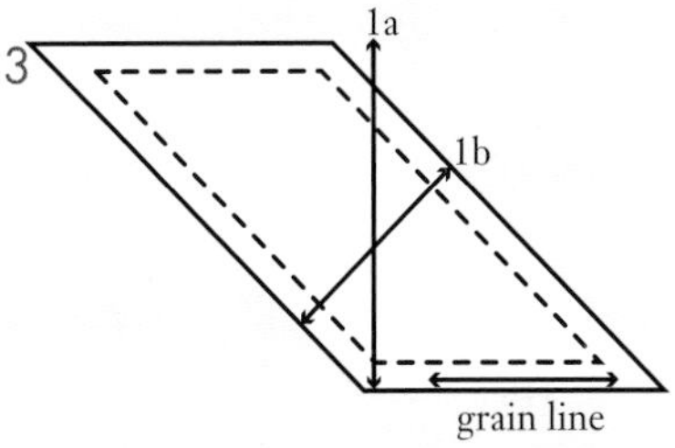

Fig. 34

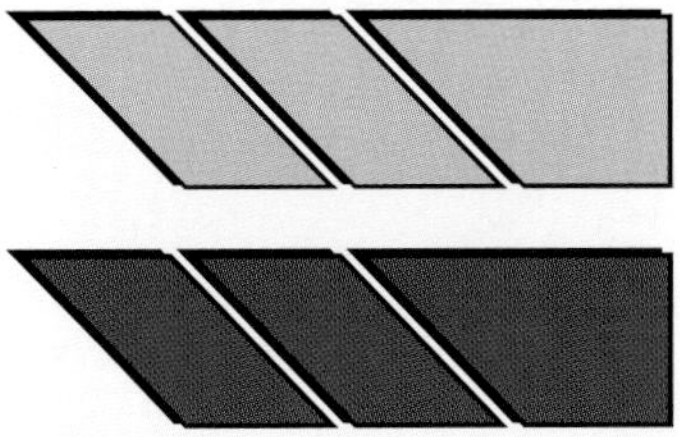

NOTE: When cutting parallelograms or diamonds from layered fabrics, the way the fabrics are layered will determine which position they take when sewn together. The figure on the left was cut with the light fabric on top while the figure on the right was cut with the dark fabric on top.

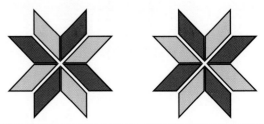

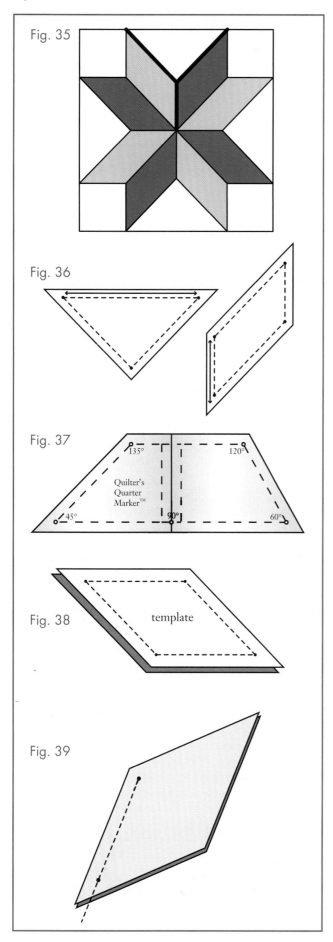

Fig. 35

Fig. 36

Fig. 37

Quilter's
Quarter
Marker™

135° 120°
45° 90° 60°

Fig. 38

template

Fig. 39

Y-seam construction

(Fig. 35) Y-seams occur in blocks containing parallelograms and diamonds as well as inset triangles and squares. Y-seams are named for the shpae created by the two diagonal seams and single straight seam. The darkened lines in Figure 35 show the Y-shape.

(Fig. 36) Notice the dark dots in the corners of template pieces that will be inset. These marks are exactly ¼" from the edges of the template. These seam intersection marks should be transferred to the back of the fabric to eliminate guesswork.

Before marking the patches, cut a template for the individual shape. With a large needle, punch small holes in the template where the small dots appear on the template patterns. The hole has to be large enough to accommodate a pencil tip or fine point permanent pen.

(Fig. 37) Some marking tools have holes placed at the correct points for the angles most commonly used by quilters (see Resources, page 110, for the author's preferences).

(Fig. 38) After cutting the pieces by strip method or template, mark through the holes onto the back of the fabric by aligning the template or tool with the corresponding corner or point of the patch. Insert a sharp dark pencil or permanent pen through the hole and twist it to mark the fabric.

All of the illustrations for sewing Y-seams will be shown with diamonds and triangles, although the steps are the same when squares are inset or parallelograms are sewn.

Sewing inset seams

(Fig. 39) Sew pairs of diamonds or parallelograms together first. Align a pair of diamonds so your sewing machine needle will enter the fabric right at the mark. Bring the needle down into the fabric. Take one stitch forward and one back. Then sew forward off the edge of the fabric.

Set-in triangles or squares

(Fig. 40) Align the mark on the square or triangle with the mark at the beginning of the seam.

(Fig. 41) Start sewing at the seam between the diamonds. Backstitch. Be sure the other diamond is pulled out of the way and will not be caught in the new seam. Take one stitch forward and one back, then sew the seam.

Remove the patches from the machine. Pivot the triangle or square so that the unsewn edge aligns with the second diamond. Gently pull the first diamond out of the way and hold it while sewing the seam.

(Fig. 42) Take one stitch at the beginning of the first seam, backstitch once, and then sew the length of the seam and off the other end.

(Fig. 43) Place the piece face up. Press the seam allowances between the inset piece and the diamonds toward the diamonds. Then press the seam allowance between the diamonds under the darker fabric. Trim the protruding points.

QUICK PIECING

A number of the projects in this book call for pieced units like half-square triangles, quarter-square triangles, Flying Geese, and more. Cutting and handling individual pieces to make these units can be time-consuming and tedious. On the following pages are charts showing examples of quick piecing methods to make easy work of piecing these common units.

MARKING PIECES: Sewing lines are marked on the wrong side of the pieces. Use a .05 mechanical pencil with soft lead to draw lines because the point is consistently fine. Or use a fine point permanent ink pen in a color that shows on the wrong side but doesn't bleed through the fabric. (See Resources, page 110, for the author's preferences.)

As an alternative, you may find a ½" wide marking tool helpful when marking pieces for the quick piecing methods shown here (see the Resources section, page 110, for the author's preference). If using a marking tool, sew on the drawn line.

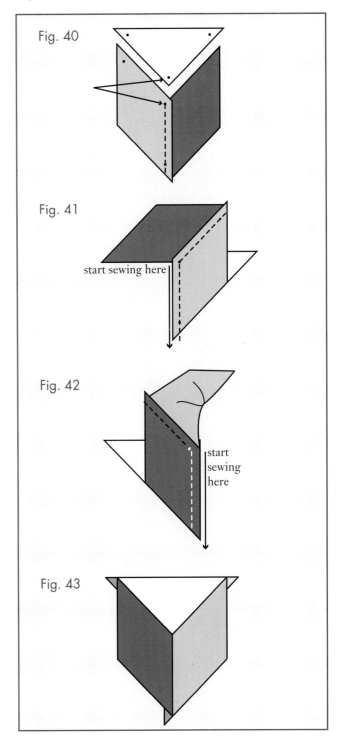

Fig. 40

Fig. 41

start sewing here

Fig. 42

start sewing here

Fig. 43

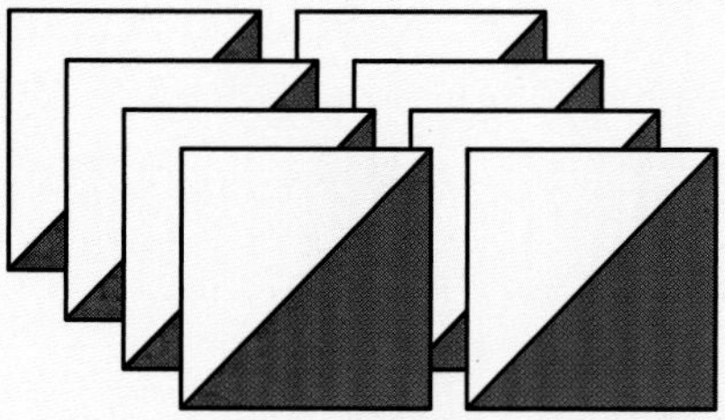

HALF-SQUARE TRIANGLES – *MULTIPLES* (HSTM)

The exact sizes of the squares you'll need are given with each pattern. To do the math for your own blocks, take the finished size of the patch and add ⅞" for seam allowances, then multiply that number by two. Cut two squares that size, each of a different fabric to yield eight half-square triangle units. A 4" finished half-square triangle unit is shown as a construction example.

Finished size (FS)	Cut 2 squares FS + ⅞" x 2
4"	9¾"

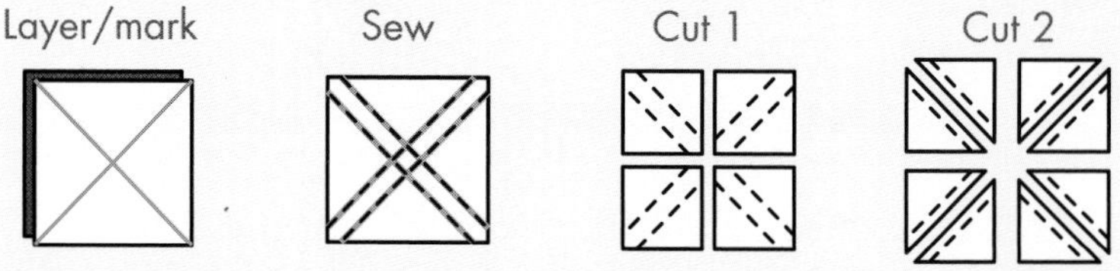
Layer/mark
Sew
Cut 1
Cut 2

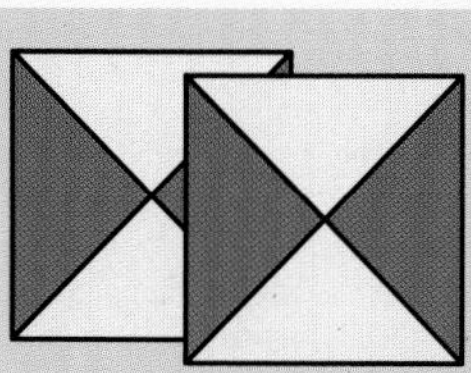

PIECED QUARTER-SQUARE TRIANGLES (QST)

These directions use two different fabrics. The exact sizes of the squares you'll need to cut are given with each pattern. To do the math for your own blocks, take the finished size of the unit and add 1¼" to that amount. Cut one square from each fabric. This method yields two quarter-square triangle units. A 4" unit is shown as an example.

Finished Size (FS)	Cut 2 squares FS + 1¼"
4"	5¼"

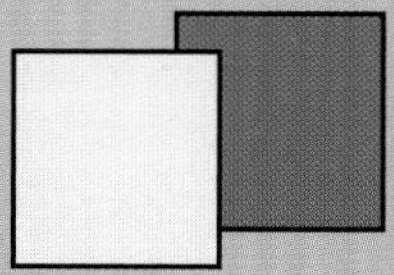

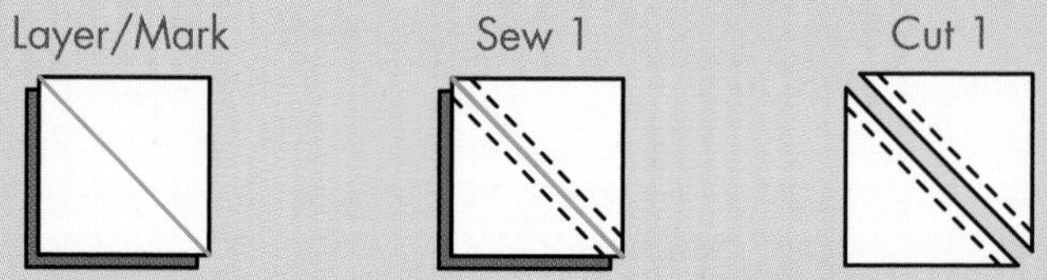
Layer/Mark
Sew 1
Cut 1

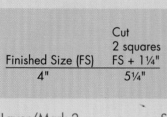

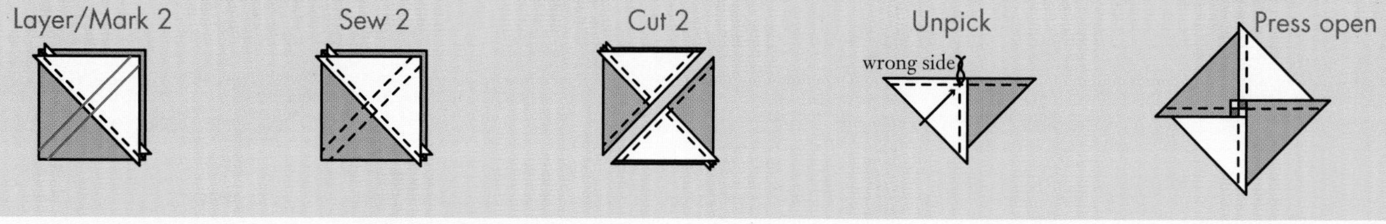
Layer/Mark 2
Sew 2
Cut 2
Unpick
wrong side
Press open

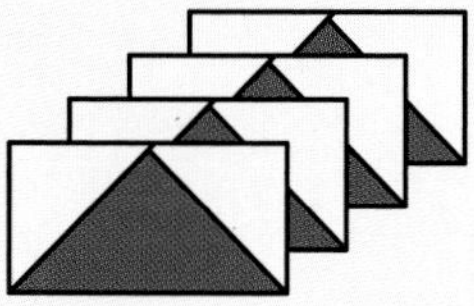

FLYING GEESE (FG)

These Flying Geese units are made using two different fabrics and two sizes of squares and there is no waste. The exact sizes of the squares are given with each pattern. To do the math for your own blocks, take the finished width of the Flying Geese unit and add 1¼" for seam allowances. Cut one square that size. The finished height of a Flying Geese unit is half its width. Add ⅞" for seam allowances and cut four squares that size from a different fabric. Yields four Flying Geese units. A 4" x 2" Flying Geese unit is shown as an example.

Finished Size (FS)	Cut 1 square FS width + 1¼"	Cut 4 squares ½ FS width + ⅞"
4" x 2"	5¼"	2⅞"

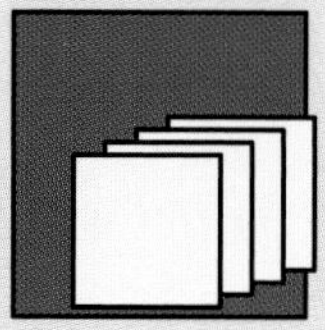

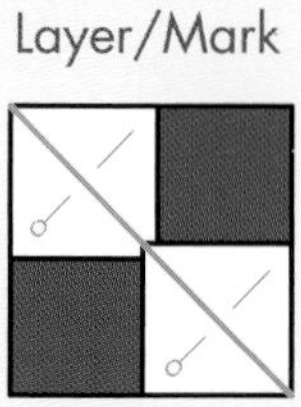
Layer/Mark

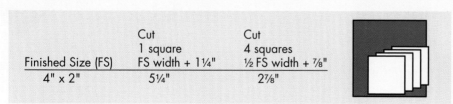

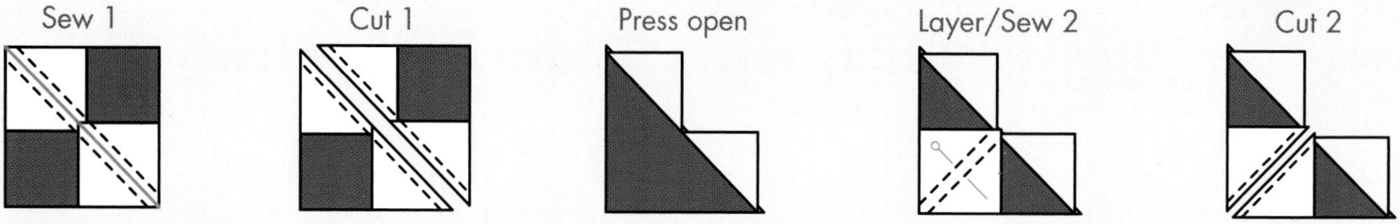
Sew 1
Cut 1
Press open
Layer/Sew 2
Cut 2

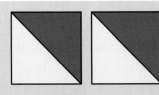

HALF-SQUARE TRIANGLES – *PAIRS* (HSTP)

The exact sizes of squares you'll need are given with each pattern. To do the math for your own blocks, take the finished size of the patch and add ⅞" for seam allowances. Cut two squares that size, each of a different fabric, to yield two pieced half-square triangles. A 4" finished half-square triangle unit is shown as a construction example.

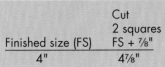

Finished size (FS)	Cut 2 squares FS + ⅞"	
4"	4⅞"	

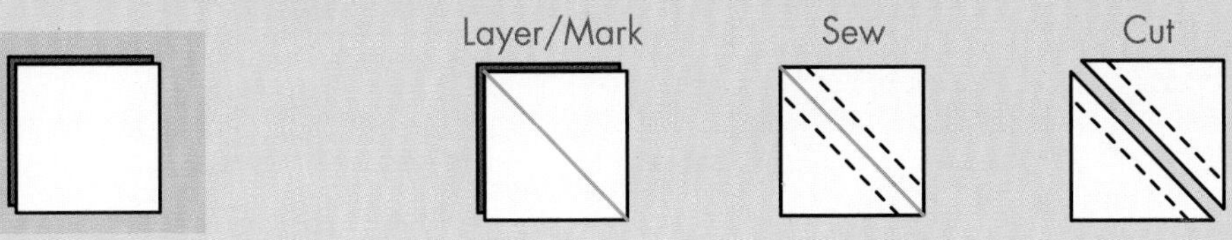

Layer/Mark   Sew   Cut

SQUARE ON-POINT (SqP)

This unit is made from squares of two different fabrics. There is no waste because when trimming, you get four bonus half-square triangles for later use. The exact sizes of the squares you'll need to cut are given with each pattern. To do the math for your own blocks, take the finished size of the patch and add 1¼" for seam allowances. Cut one square that size. The finished height of the small triangles is half the width of the block. Add ⅞" for seam allowances and cut four small squares that size from another fabric. A 4" block is shown as an example. This method yields one square on-point unit and four pieced half-square triangles.

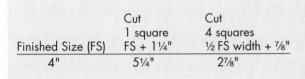

Finished Size (FS)	Cut 1 square FS + 1¼"	Cut 4 squares ½ FS width + ⅞"
4"	5¼"	2⅞"

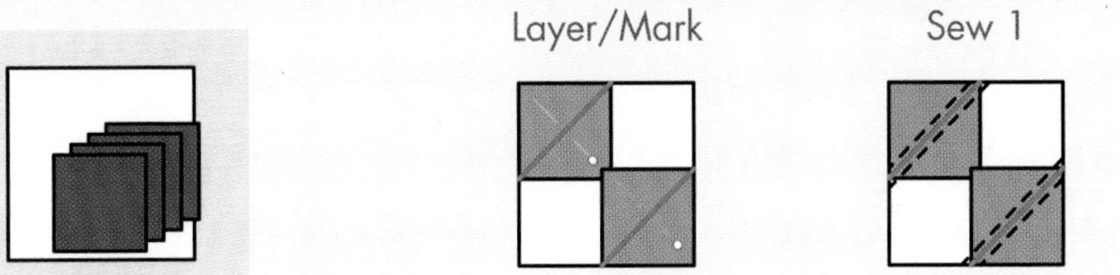

Layer/Mark   Sew 1

   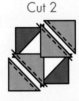

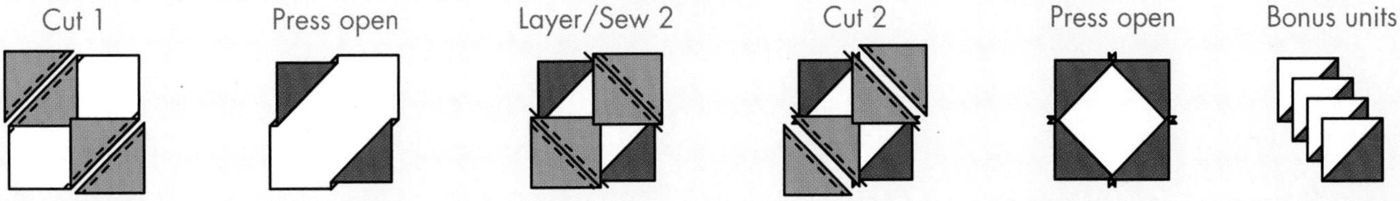

Cut 1   Press open   Layer/Sew 2   Cut 2   Press open   Bonus units

FOUR-PATCH ON-POINT (FPP)

This unit combines two quick piecing techniques – those of square on-point and quarter-square triangles. The sizes of the squares you'll need to cut are given with each pattern. To do the math for your own units, take the finished size of the patch and add 2" to that amount. Cut two squares that size, each from a different fabric. For the corner triangles, cut four squares half the size of the finished unit plus ⅞" from a third fabric.

Finished size (FS)	Cut 2 squares FS + 2"	Cut 4 squares ½ FS + ⅞"
4"	6"	2⅞"

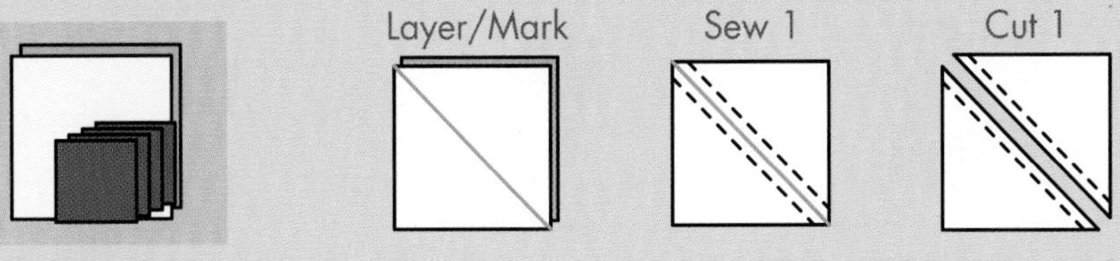

NOTE: You can also make this unit using three or four fabrics. Save the bonus units trimmed off after the third sewing step for later use.

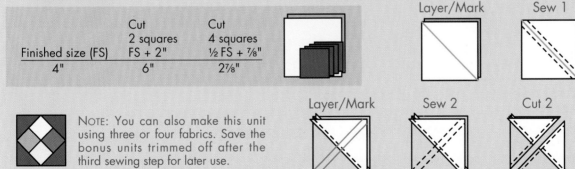

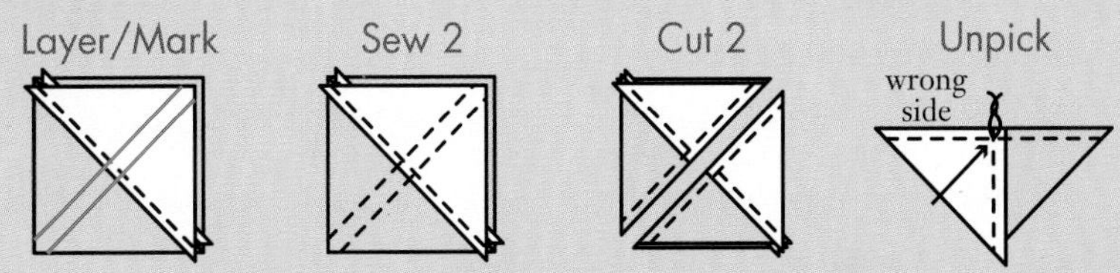

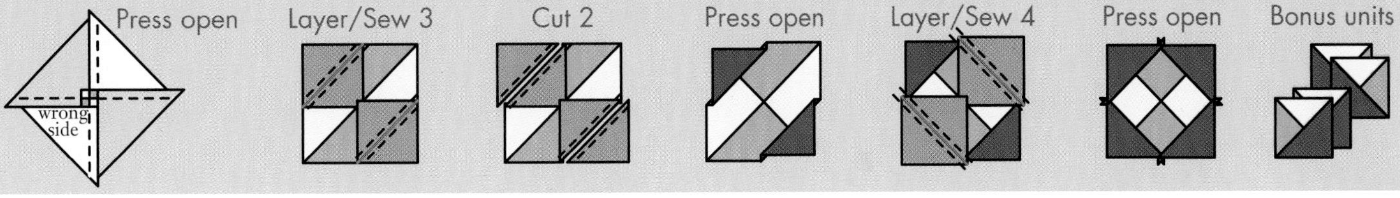

Layer/Mark   Sew 1   Cut 1

Layer/Mark   Sew 2   Cut 2   Unpick

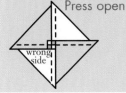

Press open   Layer/Sew 3   Cut 2   Press open   Layer/Sew 4   Press open   Bonus units

Setting and Corner Triangles

SETTING TRIANGLES: Every deep indentation in the outer edge of a diagonal pieced quilt requires a triangle to fill in the space.

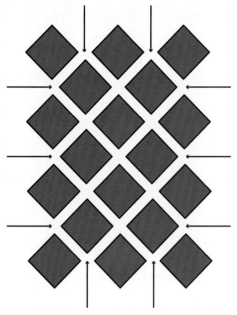

In order to have the straight of grain on the outside edge of the quilt, setting triangles are cut from squares. The square is cut twice diagonally. These triangles cannot be used for the corners since the grainline on the outside edge would be bias and would tend to distort.

CORNER TRIANGLES: Corners are also cut from squares but in order to preserve the straight of grain on the outside edges of the quilt, the square is cut in half once diagonally.

Setting Triangles   Corner Triangles

BORDERS

Unless otherwise indicated, cut all border strips from the lengthwise fabric grain (parallel to the selvage). This grain has very little or no stretch. Cutting borders on the lengthwise grain requires more fabric, but the borders are less likely to ripple.

Borders with straight cut corners

Measure the height of the quilt top through the center. This measurement is used to cut the border strips for the sides of the quilt. The amount of this measurement is specified in each pattern.

> NOTE: The horizontal strips should not be cut until after the side borders are attached.

(Fig. 44) Fold the strips and the quilt into quarters (a very large quilt should be folded into eighths). Match the fold points as indicated by the Xs. Pin each strip and the quilt together at the ends and at each fold point. Sew the seam with the quilt on top. However, if the quilt has some stretch along the edges, it is best to sew with the border strip on top.

(Fig. 45) Measure the width of the quilt, including the side borders. Cut border strips for the top and bottom of the quilt to the width you have measured. Fold, pin, and sew the strips as before.

Borders with mitered corners

To make mitered borders, the strips are cut longer than the quilt measurement. Each border strip for a mitered border must include the height (or width) of the quilt top plus the width of the borders.

Measure the quilt through the center in both directions – height and width. To find the amount needed for the miter, take the cut width of the border strip and multiply by 2. Then

Joining border strips

If there isn't enough fabric for a seamless border strip, join pieces with diagonal seams. Diagonal seams are less obtrusive than horizontal seams. In order to reduce the number of seams in a border, do not use less than a yard of fabric when cutting border strips.

Cut the ends of the strips to be joined at 45° angles in the same direction. Layer and cut all of the strips face up or face down.

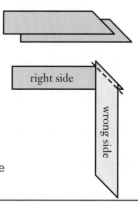

Only one end of the beginning and ending strip in a joined border needs to be cut at 45° angles.

Sew the strips together, aligning the diagonal cuts so the points protrude. Sew into and out of the "V" that is formed.

right side

wrong side

add 2" to that figure. Add that amount to the height and width measurements of the quilt top. Cut two strips for each measurement.

Take the original measurement of the quilt top and divide that amount in half. Fold the side border strips in half and finger press the crease.

(Fig. 46) From the fold, measure off half of the quilt top's measurement in both directions. Make a mark at those points with an appropriate fabric marker. Fold the quilt in half. With right sides together, align this fold with the fold of the border. Pin the edges in place.

Start sewing with a backstitch ¼" from the marks on the border strip. If you've measured and marked properly, this will also be ¼" from the edge of the quilt top. Stop with a backstitch ¼" from the mark at the opposite end. Repeat on the opposite side.

When attaching the top and bottom borders, start with a backstitch at the point where the side border seam ended, and stop with a backstitch at the other border seam. These points are seam intersections.

(Fig. 47) Remove the quilt top from the machine. Fold the quilt top diagonally from the corner with right sides together and align the outside edges of the border strips.

Mark, sew, and cut one mitered corner at a time. Align the 45° line of the ruler with the outside edge of the border strips and the ¼" line of the ruler with the seam intersection. The edge of the ruler will be at the edge of the ¼" seam allowance for the miter. Draw a line along the edge of the ruler.

(Fig. 48) Stabilize the strips by pinning on both sides of the line before moving it to the machine.

(Fig. 49) Start sewing at the seam intersection a quarter inch from the drawn line, backstitch, and sew to the outer corner.

Open the quilt and check to make sure that the miter is correct. If it is, trim the excess border with a rotary cutter. Repeat the steps for the remaining corners. Press the miter seam allowances in one direction. Press the seam allowances for the border toward the border fabric.

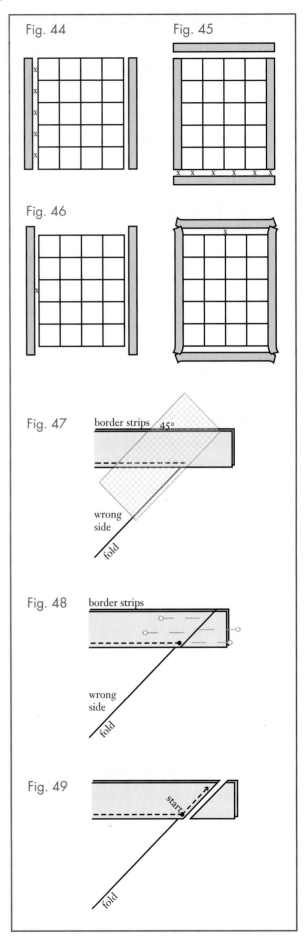

Fig. 44 Fig. 45

Fig. 46

Fig. 47 border strips 45° wrong side fold

Fig. 48 border strips wrong side fold

Fig. 49 start fold

Layering

Tape the backing, wrong side up, to a large flat surface (I use 1" or 2" wide blue painter's masking tape). Tape down the corners, then place several pieces of tape along all edges. The backing should lie flat, without puckers, but not be stretched tightly. Mark the backing edge centers with a pin or an indelible pen. Only a small dot is necessary. If your flat surface is not large enough for the whole backing to be stretched out, tape the top edge of the backing down as far as the edge of the surface and allow the rest to hang to the floor.

Center the batting over the backing and smooth it out.

Mark the quilt top edge centers with a pin or a small dot made with an indelible pen. Fold the quilt top in half with right sides together and then fold it in half the other direction. Align the quilt top with one corner of the batting, about 2" from both edges.

Unfold the quilt top. The center edge marks should line up with the center edge marks on the backing. Smooth out the quilt top without stretching.

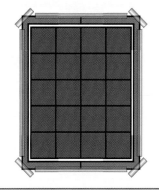

MARKING, BACKING, LAYERING, AND BASTING

Marking the quilt top

There are many marking tools available for marking quilting designs.

Large blocks of space can be marked after the quilt is basted, but you may prefer to mark beforehand. Since I wash all of my quilts after they are quilted and bound, I like to use blue water soluble pens to mark light fabrics when hand quilting. I use purple fadeaway markers when machine quilting. Use thin slivers of white hand soap or white or silver pencils on dark fabrics. Test your markers on your fabrics before using them.

Do not iron a quilt top or block after using a blue wash-away or purple fade-away pen. Though the marks may temporarily disappear, the heat may cause them to reappear later. Rinse the piece in cold water and hang it to dry.

Avoid ironing when using any kind of graphite, silver, white, or colored pencil. These markers may contain wax that sets when ironed. Wash your test scraps with a dab of quilt-safe soap. Rinse and hang to dry.

When the quilt is ready to be washed, rinse it twice in cold water to remove any chemicals, then add quilt soap to the water.

Backing and batting

It may be necessary to piece the backing for your quilt. Each project gives my recommendations for a lengthwise or crosswise seam in the backing. Do not sew selvage edges together for a backing seam; that makes the seam too thick.

There are many types of battings available. Your quilt's intended use and your quilting preference will help you choose. I prefer low loft 100% cotton or cotton/poly battings since they lend themselves to either hand or machine quilting.

Basting

Baste, using your choice of basting with thread or with 1" rustproof safety pins. There is also an adhesive basting spray that can be sprayed over the batting, and when the quilt is spread out over it, the layers will hold together.

THREAD BASTING: Thread basting should be used only when hand quilting since the presser foot will catch the threads while machine quilting. Use only 100% cotton thread and a long needle. Pull the thread off the spool to a length slightly more than enough to reach from the center of the quilt top to the edge. Do not cut the thread. Thread your needle.

(Fig. 50) Start basting at the center of the quilt and take long stitches (about 1"). Baste horizontally, then vertically to the edges. Leave a tail of thread about 5" long at the edge. Unwind more thread from the spool to reach the opposite edge. Baste diagonal lines between the first rows of stitches. The lines of basting should not be more than 3" to 4" apart.

Fold the excess backing to the front, over the batting, tucking the raw edge under. Baste the folded backing around the edges of the quilt.

PIN BASTING: Start at the center of the quilt top, placing pins horizontally and vertically, about 4" apart. Pin one quarter of the quilt top at a time and try to place pins so they will not be in the path of the presser foot as you machine quilt.

BASTING SPRAYS: Before using any basting spray, be sure to read the directions on the can to make sure it is designed for quilt basting.

Before spraying, sew a long basting stitch with white thread by hand through the middle of the batting in both directions. This will help line up the quilt top, back, and batting.

NOTE: To help make basting easier, curved basting or upholstery needles are available. Or you could use the bowl of an old spoon to "scoop" up the point of the needle as you take long basting stitches.

Fig. 50

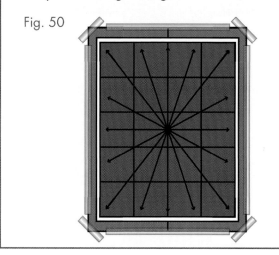

One brand of basting spray tells you to spray the fabric, another recommends spraying the batting. My preference is to spray the batting. Spray lightly when using basting spray. You do not want a heavy layer.

Do not attempt to start quilting immediately after spraying. Whether hand or machine quilting, allow the quilt to rest, unfolded, for at least 48 hours before quilting or your needle will gum up.

QUILTING

Quilting lends depth and dimension to a quilt. Quilting stitches create shadows and designs as light plays across them. These quilting stitches are also practical because they hold all three layers together.

There are many sources for quilting designs – magazines, books, quilting stencils, and even shapes found around the house or in nature.

If you are making a quilt that is straight patchwork, you might think of curved quilting designs to soften the straight lines. Use curved designs in plain blocks that are offset with patchwork blocks. Many continuous line quilting designs for machine quilting are perfect for hand quilting too.

Then there is the decision to hand or machine quilt. For me, if I have done any hand appliqué on a quilt, I will quilt by hand. If my quilt is all machine patchwork, then it usually will be machine quilted. Those decisions vary, of course, depending on why and for whom the quilt is being made.

Although overall quilting was the choice in many antique quilts, I prefer to limit overall quilting to the plain blocks or background areas of each patchwork block. I find that overall quilting, whether by hand or machine, hides the beauty of the patchwork. So, if you are having a quilt quilted on a longarm machine, try to have it done so the patchwork will not be obliterated. Perhaps she could quilt the setting strips and borders separately with a continuous design in each block. Talk to the quilter and let her know what you want.

Patchwork blocks can be quilted in the ditch by hand or machine. This means it is quilted along the seam line of the background next to the patches. This emphasizes the patchwork design, giving it depth. If you are machine quilting, you can usually use a presser foot designed for darning. If the quilt isn't too large, quilting can also be done with a walking foot as you will be turning at every corner of the patchwork.

Finding a border design that fits perfectly is often difficult. When I find a border design that I really like, I work from both ends of each side, adjusting the design in the center. This gives the best results and all four sides will look the same on a square quilt. If you have a rectangular quilt, then make sure the opposing sides are the same. Whether square or rectangular, the corners will be identical.

Another way to plan a border design is to use a piece of shelf or freezer paper cut to the length of the border. The paper can be folded or marked at even increments, then the design traced on each increment. When the paper is unfolded, the design will fit the space. Cut shapes from template plastic to fit the increments, or mark the stencil where it will fit into the increments.

Machine quilting

Machine quilting is something that you can only learn by doing. You cannot machine quilt without either a walking foot, also called an even feed foot, or a darning foot. Straight lines are easy to achieve with the walking foot, but if you want to do free-form quilting, you must have a darning foot. Start with small pieces, place mats, table runners, or wallhangings and work up to a bed-sized quilt. You will learn to work with the rhythm of your machine. I recommend taking a class from an experienced machine quilter – you'll learn valuable tips.

Hand quilting

Whether you work on a large frame, on a hoop, or in your lap, some techniques are the same. The quilt should be held flat but should not be as tight as a drum inside the frame or hoop. The quilt needs to have some give so that as you push up from beneath with a finger or thimble, a ridge can be formed.

THIMBLES: I use three thimbles when quilting. Since I am right-handed, a thimble on my right middle finger pushes the needle through the fabric. I prefer an open nail thimble (Fig. 51).

(Fig. 52) I also wear a finger protector over my left index and middle fingers. My left hand is beneath the quilt and as I push the needle through the fabric, the finger protector creates a ridge in the quilt that deflects the point of the needle. My finger protector is metal and using it aids in making even stitches (see Resources, pg. 110).

I cut a finger from a rubber glove for my right thumb. This helps me grasp the needle to pull it through the three layers. These fingers wear out as you use them, but a pair of rubber kitchen gloves will provide you with an ample supply.

QUILTING NEEDLES: The needles most often used for quilting are quilting betweens. The higher the number, the finer and shorter the needle. The shorter the needle you use, the smaller your stitches will be. If you are a beginner, you might want to start with a #8 or #9 needle, but try to work toward using a #10 or #12.

QUILTING STITCH: This stitch is basically a running stitch. The evenness of the quilting stitches is more important than the size. As you develop skill in keeping the stitches even, the stitch size will also diminish.

(Fig. 53) Cut a piece of thread no longer than 18" and make a knot at one end. Begin at a seam allowance by inserting the needle and thread through only the top layer and the seam allowance.

Bring the needle through the front of the quilt top where you want to take the first quilting stitch. Gently, but firmly, pull the knot through the top layer, burying the knot and tail in the seam allowance.

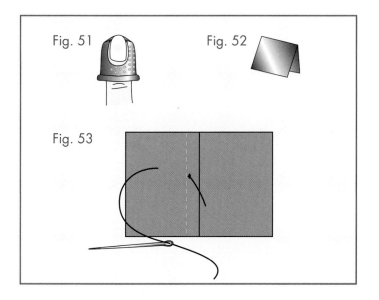

Fig. 51

Fig. 52

Fig. 53

(Fig. 54) Use a rocking motion, pushing the needle with the thimble on your right hand through the quilt and against the thimble underneath. Take the first stitch, and when you see the glint of the needle point, rock the finger back so the point is then pushed through again. Do not take more than three or four stitches on the needle at one time, depending on the thickness of the batting.

Pull the thread up firmly, so the thread is buried in the fabric. This brings the backing, batting, and quilt top together. The fabric should not gather as you pull up the stitches.

Insert the needle into the fabric again, about the same distance away as the length of the stitches that you've already made. Repeat the process.

ENDING THE THREAD: (Fig. 55) End the thread when there is still about 2" to 3" in the needle.

Wrap the tail of thread around the stitches that hold the three layers together. To do this, after taking the last stitch, slip the needle through the top layer back along the row of stitches the length of about 4 or 5 stitches. Bring the needle up at the end of a stitch about half of the needle's length.

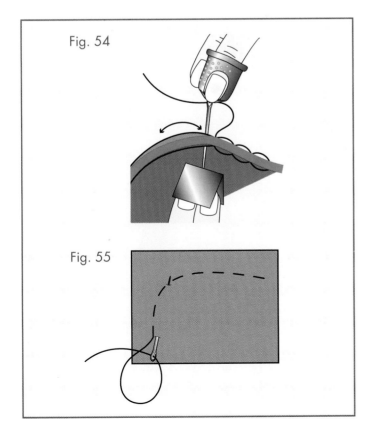

Fig. 54

Fig. 55

Pull the needle and thread through, go back down at the same place where the needle came up, but now slide the needle the length of one or two stitches along the other side of the row of stitches. Bring the needle out of the quilt top again at the end of one of the stitches.

Repeat the last two steps, then bring the needle out away from the stitches and pull it through. The tail can be swept under the quilt top or clipped off.

This section covers only a very basic way to quilt. There are many books available that are devoted to perfecting quilt stitches.

FINISHING AND BINDING

Preparing your quilt for binding
The easiest type of binding to attach and sew is a double fold or French fold binding.

Prepare your quilt for binding by squaring the edges. Using a rotary cutter and ruler, trim the batting and backing of the quilt on all sides.

Cutting the Binding
If the fabric in the quilt has been preshrunk, preshrink the binding as well. Binding can be cut across the fabric, from selvage to selvage or cut the length of the fabric. Unless there are curves along the edge of your quilt, do not use bias strips. Bias stretches easily and is a major cause of ripples along the quilt edges.

Binding cut across the width of the fabric does have some stretch and if not applied with care can also cause ripples. One advantage to binding cut across the width of the quilt is that only a small amount of fabric is required.

Binding cut on the lengthwise grain of the fabric has very little or no stretch. To cut down on the number of seams in the binding, purchase at least one yard of fabric. There may be a large amount of fabric leftover after cutting, especially for narrow binding. If the fabric used in the binding will also appear in the quilt top, allow for an extra amount in the original purchase. Cut the binding strips before cutting the patches. The binding width for each quilt is listed with each project.

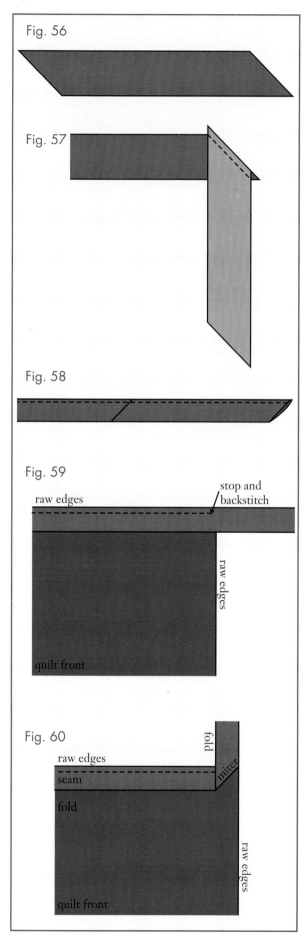

Fig. 56

Fig. 57

Fig. 58

Fig. 59

raw edges

stop and backstitch

raw edges

quilt front

Fig. 60

fold

raw edges

seam

miter

fold

raw edges

quilt front

CUTTING ON LENGTHWISE GRAIN: If cutting binding strips lengthwise from a yard of fabric, divide the perimeter measurement of the quilt by 36". For example, if the perimeter measurement of the quilt is 168", your math will tell you that 4.6 strips are needed. Since .6 is over half a strip, cut six strips the desired width.

Always cut an extra strip if the amount is a small fraction of a strip. If the amount is over half a strip, cut two extra.

CUTTING ON CROSSWISE GRAIN: If cutting binding strips across the width of standard 42" wide fabric, divide the perimeter measurement of the quilt by 42".

Again, if the perimeter measurement is 168", the math will indicate that exactly four strips are required. But cut one extra (a total of five strips) to allow for joins and mitering.

Preparing the Binding
(Fig. 56) Cut the strips then trim both ends at a 45° angle. Layer and cut all of the strips either face up or face down and always cut the angles in the same direction.

(Fig. 57) With right sides together, join the strips using a ¼" seam allowance. Sew into and out of the "V" where the points protrude. Press the seam allowances open to reduce bulk. Trim protrusions.

(Fig. 58) Fold the strip in half lengthwise with wrong sides together. Match the edges and press the fold.

Sewing the Binding to the Quilt
Start at a midway point on one side. Leave a tail of binding about 10" long. Align the raw edges of the binding along the raw edges of the quilt and sew to the corner.

(Fig. 59) Remove the quilt from the machine. Lay the corner flat.

(Fig. 60) Fold the binding so a miter forms at the corner.

(Fig. 61) Next, fold the binding so a fold forms along the top edge of the quilt and the raw edges are in line with the right edge of the quilt. The miter will be hidden underneath. Sew from that corner to the next corner.

Repeat on each side of the quilt. On the last side, backstitch about 12" from the beginning point, waiting to trim. Remove the quilt from the machine and lay it on a flat surface.

Closing the Binding

(Fig. 62) Bring the loose ends of the binding approximately to the center of the unsewn edge.

(Fig. 63) Open the bindings. At approximately the center point where the loose bindings meet, mark the beginning piece with a 45° line. Cut off the excess at the diagonal line.

(Fig. 64) Bring the beginning piece over the end piece. Mark a diagonal line on the end, matching it with the diagonal edge of the beginning piece. Mark another line ½" from the first line for the seam allowance. Cut the excess off the ending piece.

(Fig. 65) With right sides together, join the bindings using a ¼" seam allowance. Finish sewing the binding in place.

(Fig. 66) Turn the quilt over so the back is facing up. At the corners, fold the right side first and fold the top binding over it, so that the right side is tucked underneath. Placing a pin horizontal to the edge of the quilt as shown might help keep the fold and corner sharp.

Tuck in the binding and corner of the quilt. The binding will automatically miter. If there is too much bulk, trim out a small amount of the quilt top, backing, and batting. The miter folds should lie opposite those on the front side so the bulk is reduced.

Sew the fold by hand, just covering the machine stitched seam on the back. Stitch the miters in place at the same time.

NOTE: If you are attaching a ¼" binding, sew ¼" from the raw edges and stop ¼" from the corner. For a ½" binding, sew a ½" seam and stop ½" from the corner. Whatever the finished width should be, that is the seam allowance.

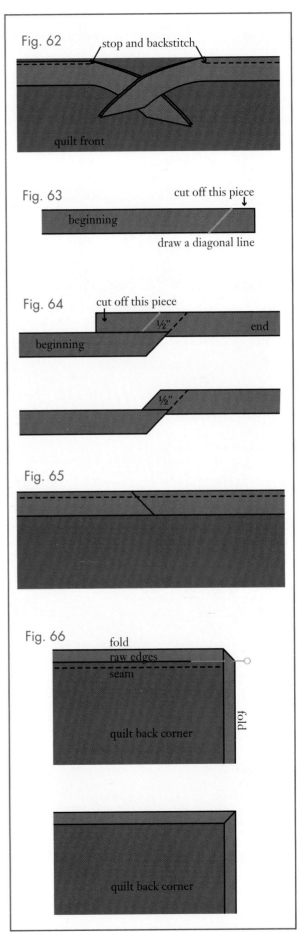

DELECTABLE MOUNTAIN

In the book *Pilgrim's Progress*, I remember this one part:

"They went then till they came to the Delectable Mountain. Behold the gardens and orchards, the vineyards and fountains of water..."

That's how I think of our mountain, so I made this quilt.

John brought me to this place. As we stood here together, I could see across the valley to the blue mountain ridges. The valley was awash in orange, yellow, and purple wildflowers. We dreamed and planned – this was where we would build our home and our family would grow. I wanted a big window in the front room. It would be good light for the quilt frame. John made that frame for me.

The brown woods, green leaves, and wildflowers were the summer colors around me, but winter was the best time for quilting. On those winter days the stove would be stoked with firewood John had cut through the summer. I worked at the frame. Sometimes John would thread the needles for me as I quilted or he read to us. Often the children played a game or did their school work.

I'd put on a pot of soup to simmer – a ham bone, onion, herbs from the garden, maybe some beans. Other times there'd be a stewing hen or even a rabbit with carrots and potatoes. In this way I cooked for my family and quilted at the same time.

Barbara Dieges

Finished size: 55½" x 71½"
Finished block size: 8⅛"
Number of blocks: 48

Setting: 6 x 8 blocks
Alternate settings shown on pg. 31

Barbara Dieges

Amount/Fabric	Piece/Amount	1st Cut	2nd Cut	Assembly
12 Fat Quarters – Dark and med. prints/plaids	**Half-square Triangles** – 336 4 from each fabric **Small Triangles** – 96 8 from each fabric **Medium Triangles** – 48 4 from each fabric	(1) 5" strip (1) 2½" strip (2) 5¾" squares	(4) 5" squares (4) 2½" squares Once diagonally	(HSTM – pg. 18) Cut once diagonally
12 Fat Quarters – Lt. prints	**Half-square Triangles** – 336 4 from each fabric **Large Triangles** – 48 4 from each fabric	(1) 5" strip (2) 9" squares	(4) 5" squares Once diagonally	(HSTM – pg. 18)
1⅞ yd. – Light/med. prints	**Inner Border**	(2) 2⅛" strips x top length (2) 2⅛" strips x top width		
2 yds. – Dark print	**Outer Border**	(2) 3¾" x top length (2) 3¾" x top width		
1 yd. – Dark	**Binding**	(9) 2¾" strips on lengthwise grain		
3¾ yds.	**Backing**	Seam across the width of the quilt		
60" x 76"	**Batting**			

This quilt has many different fabrics. Two fat quarters, one each of dark and light, are enough for four blocks. Randomly place blocks for a scrappy look.

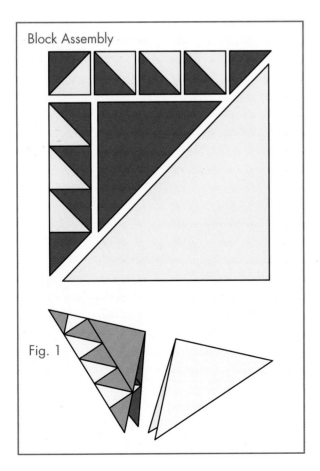

Block Assembly

Fig. 1

Block Assembly

Make 336 half-square triangles from the 5" squares using the multiples method of construction shown on pg. 18.

There will be one extra finished half-square triangle from each sewn square. Some of these units are used for the border corners. Save the others for another project.

Match the fabrics of the units and triangles in each block, then assemble as shown in the Block Assembly diagram.

(Fig. 1) After sewing the side of the block containing half-square triangles, fold it and the large triangle in half. Crease at the fold, then with right sides together match the creases and corners. Pin and sew together.

Settings

The possible settings for Delectable Mountain blocks are numerous. Some alternate possibilities are shown in Figures 2 and 3.

Inner border

Measure the height and width of the quilt top, it should measure 49¼" x 65½", including seam allowances.

From light fabric, cut two, 2⅛" strips to your height measurement for the sides, and two, 2⅛" strips to your width measurement for the top and bottom borders.

Pin and sew the side strips to the quilt top (see the Quilt Assembly diagram).

(Fig. 4) Sew a leftover half-square triangle to each end of the top and bottom strips.

Pin and sew the strips to the top and bottom of the quilt top. Abut the seam allowances of the added squares (see the Quilt Assembly diagram).

Outer border

Measure the height and width of the quilt top. It should measure 52½" x 68¾". Trim the 3¾" outer border strips to the actual measurements.

Pin and sew the side strips to the quilt top (see the Quilt Assembly diagram).

(Fig. 5) Make four Pinwheel blocks with 16 of the leftover half-square triangles.

(Fig. 6) Sew a Pinwheel block to each end of the top and bottom strips.

Pin and sew the strips to the top and bottom of the quilt top. Abut the seam allowances of the Pinwheel squares (see the Quilt Assembly diagram).

Quilting

(See pgs. 22 – 24 for techniques on layering, basting, and quilting.) This quilt is machine quilted using a continuous line design in each patch. The large triangles are quilted with a heart and leaves design.

Binding

This quilt has a ⅜" finished binding (see Binding, pg. 25).

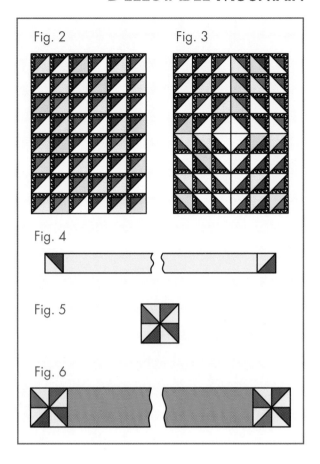

Fig. 2   Fig. 3

Fig. 4

Fig. 5

Fig. 6

Quilt Assembly

Baskets 'n Vines

I always thought I should keep a diary so I'd be able to remind myself about things that had happened. But, I was always too busy and besides, I would rather pick up some stitching.

BASKETS 'N VINES, like all my quilts, is something like a diary. Each basket is full of memories. They're bursting to tell all they know.

These days I find memories in the quilts I've made. No one else can read them, but when I look at each quilt, I remember what I was doing, what I was thinking, or what was happening at the time.

Mama sent me a big box of pieces along with a note from Granny that said she didn't think she would be using them up. There were a lot of memories in that box. When I pulled them out, there were pieces of dresses, aprons, and shirts that Granny or Mama had made. One piece made me remember Mama talking about growing up in Bavaria.

She lived with her grandparents, parents, and six brothers and sisters over the village bakery. The big oven kept the upstairs warm. My Grandma did all the sewing in that little village. When she sewed for the farmers, she was paid not with money most of the time, but with hams, eggs, milk, or cheese.

Gypsies came through the village and had babies that needed baptizing. Well, she cleaned up the babies and sewed little dresses for them. I still have some of the linens she marked with her initials – they're packed away.

All those memories…

Barbara Dieges

Finished size: 68" x 85¾"
Finished block size: 12½"
Number of blocks: 12

Setting: Three by four blocks, diagonal set, with plain alternate blocks

Barbara Dieges

Amount/Fabric	Piece/Amount	1st Cut	2nd Cut	3rd Cut
3¾ yd. – Off white	**Blocks – Background**			
	Triangles – 72	(2) 3¾" strips	(18) 3¾" squares	Twice diagonally
	Squares – 36	(2) 2¼" strips	(36) 2¼" squares	
	Triangles – 48	(2) 2⅝" strips	(24) 2⅝" squares	Once diagonally
	Rectangles – 24	(6) 2¾" strips	(24) 2¾" x 8½" rectangles	
	Triangles – 12	(6) 5⅜" squares	Once diagonally	
	Alternate blocks – 6	(2) 13" strips	(6) 13" squares	
	Setting triangles – 12	(2) 19" strips	(3) 19" squares	Twice diagonally
	Corner triangles – 4	(2) 9¾" squares	Once diagonally	
⅜ yd. (or scraps) – Green dark, medium prints and plaids	**Blocks – diamonds**			
	Make 72	(5) 1¾" strips	Cut diamonds from strips (see page 15)	
⅜ yd. (or scraps) – Red dark, medium prints and plaids	Make 72	(5) 1¾" strips	Cut diamonds from strips	
1 Fat Quarter* each of Yellow, gold, brown, or mix colors	**Blocks – Baskets**			
	Triangles – 12	(6) 6⅞" squares	Once diagonally	
	Triangles – 12	(6) 9⅜" squares	Once diagonally	
	Triangles – 24	(12) 3⅛" squares	Once diagonally	
2⅛ yds. – Dark print	**Inner Border**	(2) 1¾" x top length (2) 1¾" x top width		
2⅛ yds. – Light print	**Outer Border**	(2) 6¾" x top length (2) 6¾" x top width		
	Checkerboard Corners	(20) 1¾" x 8" rectangles		
	Outer Border Appliqué			
½ yd. – Green #1	Vine – 8 yds.	1" strips on bias		
¼ yd. – Green #2	Buds – 60	(4) 1¼" strips	30 from green/red strip units and	
¼ yd. – Red		(2) 1" strips	30 from green/yellow strip units	
¼ yd. – Yellow		(2) 1" strips		
¼ yd. – Green #3	Leaves – 82	82 shapes		
Scraps – Red, green, and yellow	**Checkerboard Corners**	(20) 1¾" strips – random amounts of each fabric		
⅝ yd. – Freezer paper	**Buds** **Leaves**	60 pieces 82 pieces		
1 yd. – Dark fabric	**Binding**	(10) 2¾" strips on lengthwise grain		
5¼ yds.	**Backing**	Seam the length of the quilt		
72" x 90"	**Batting**			

* The yardage for the baskets calls for one fat quarter each of yellow, gold, or brown. I actually used many more fabrics than that (scraps would work well). In my quilt, the small basket is a different fabric than the large one in the same block, but they could be the same.

Block Assembly

Refer to pg. 15 for helpful information on cutting diamonds, and pg. 16 for tips on sewing the diamonds and Y-seams in this quilt.

(Fig. 1) Sew the diamonds together in pairs and press seam allowances to the right.

(Figs. 2 & 3) Set in the background triangles between each pair of diamonds, then sew two diamond/background triangle units together.

(Fig. 4) Set in the background squares, making three square/diamond/triangle units for each block. Add triangles to each unit as shown in the Block Assembly diagram. Assemble 12 blocks.

Quilt top assembly

Set alternate and pieced blocks together (see the Quilt Assembly diagram). See pg. 20 for diagonal settings. Finish the appliqué borders before attaching any borders.

CHECKERBOARD CORNERS:
(Fig. 5) Sew five, 1¾" x 8" strips together – two dark and three light – to make Unit 1. Cut 16, 1¾" segments from Unit 1. Save eight Unit 1 segments to attach to both ends of each appliquéd border strip.

(Fig. 6) Sew five, 1¾" x 8" strips – three dark and two light – to make Unit 2. Press seam allowances under the dark fabric. Cut 12, 1¾" segments from Unit 2.

(Fig. 7) Alternate the segments from Unit 1 with Unit 2 segments to make four checkerboard squares.

Outer border appliqué

(See pgs. 9 – 14 for information on appliquéing.) Before cutting the appliqué border strips, measure the height and width of the quilt top and cut the pieces slightly longer than your measurements. They can be trimmed to size later after the appliqué is finished. At this point, the quilt top should measure 53½" x 71¼".

The outer border strips should be appliquéd before they are attached to the quilt top. The appliqué design for the outer borders is shown on page 37 so you can use it as a guide to position the appliqué elements on your border strips.

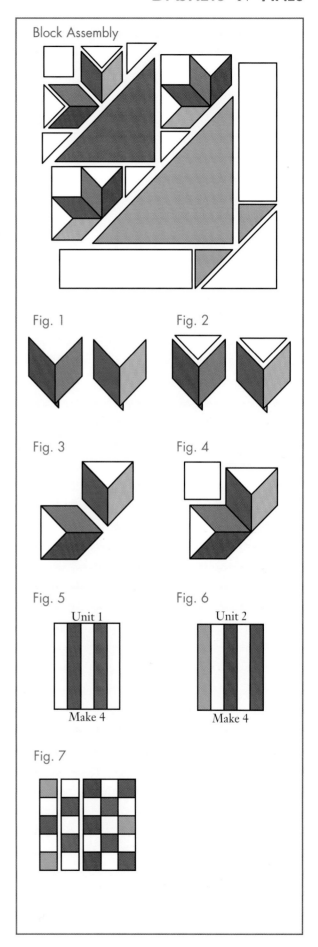

Block Assembly

Fig. 1   Fig. 2

Fig. 3   Fig. 4

Fig. 5   Fig. 6
Unit 1   Unit 2
Make 4   Make 4

Fig. 7

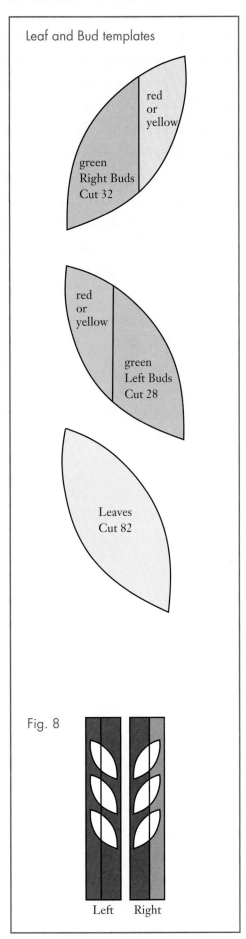

Leaf and Bud templates

red
or
yellow

green
Right Buds
Cut 32

red
or
yellow

green
Left Buds
Cut 28

Leaves
Cut 82

Fig. 8

Left   Right

Appliqué the buds, leaves, and vine according to directions in the General Instructions section.

VINES: Cut strips of 1" bias for the vines and sew the pieces together to make an 8 yard length. Fold, press, and stitch the bias following the directions for Appliqué Vine #1 on pg. 13. The vine for this project measures ¼" when finished.

BUDS: Sew a green strip to each of the yellow and red strips and press seam allowances under the green fabric.

Trace bud shapes from the templates on this page onto the dull side of freezer paper, marking the straight line. Cut 32 bud shapes angling to the right and 28 angling to the left.

(Fig. 8) Iron the freezer paper shapes with the shiny side toward the fabric to the wrong side of the sewn strips, aligning the straight line with the seam line. Make sure the buds are aligned properly with the green at the bottom.

When appliquéing the buds to the border pieces, make sure the green tip touches the vine.

LEAVES: Trace leaf shapes from the templates on this page onto the dull side of freezer paper and cut out the shapes. Space them about ½" apart on the green #3 fabric and cut out the leaves, being sure to add seam allowances as you cut.

Inner border

Measure the quilt top before cutting the border strips on the lengthwise grain of the fabric. Cut to actual measurements.

Pin and sew the 1¾" inner border strips to the sides of the quilt top after the outer border is finished. Pin and sew the inner border strips to the top and bottom.

Appliqué border

Attach two Unit 1 segments to both ends of two appliquéd border strips (see the Quilt Assembly diagram). Pin and sew the appliquéd side border strips to both sides of the quilt top.

Sew a checkerboard square to each end of the top and bottom border strips. Abut the seam allowances of the Unit 1 segment. Pin and sew the strips to the top and bottom of the quilt top (see the Quilt Assembly diagram).

Quilting
On BASKETS 'N VINES, the plain alternate blocks are machine quilted with a basket design, however a feather wreath would also be appropriate. The pieced blocks and appliqué border are quilted in the ditch.

Binding
This quilt has a ⅜" binding. See pg. 25 for information on bindings.

Quilt Assembly

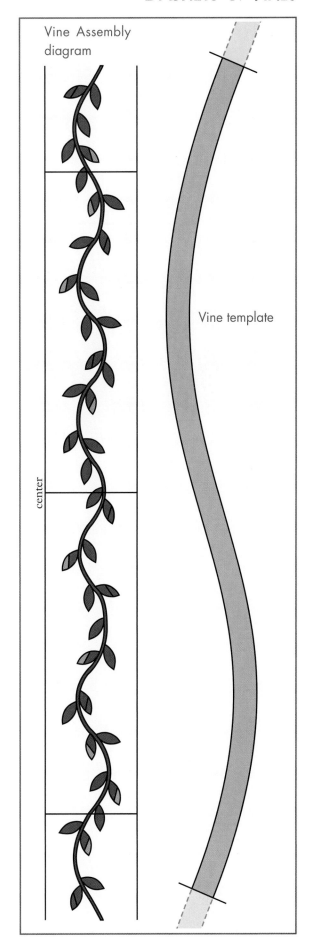

Vine Assembly diagram

center

Vine template

HOME on the MOUNTAIN

There was no school when we built our house. Then the families came and the children. We all helped to build the school in some way. The men worked together to put it up. The women cooked pots of food to feed them. Afterwards I made this quilt to remember. I think of it as HOME ON THE MOUNTAIN.

Like our village, the houses in the quilt are tucked into the hollers. There in the middle is the schoolhouse. When I made it, I didn't like the look of empty windows, so I put some of that yellow in there for the light – the light that turned on the learning in my children.

Rebecca loved school. Reading was her favorite and books became her world. She had a hunger for learning, especially about faraway places – places she dreamt she'd visit someday.

The children brought laughter. One Sunday when she was five, maybe six, Rebecca wanted to go visit her teacher. "Mama," she said, "let's go up to the schoolhouse to visit Miss Ada."

I asked her why we should go to the schoolhouse and not to Miss Ada's home.

She looked at me with wide eyes, "Home? She has a home? She doesn't live at the schoolhouse?" Interesting. Now Rebecca's a school teacher, too.

Ethan was a handful at school. He did a lot of sitting in the chair in the corner. He even warned Lily about "that" chair. When she came home after her first day at school, she said, "Mama, it's just an old chair!" Who knows what she thought it was going to be.

One never knows what goes on in children's minds. Ethan asked about the lady from Boston that visited our neighbors. Would she always talk like that? Could she be cured?

A Thread *runs* through it

Barbara Dieges

Finished size: 60" x 60"
Finished block size: 9"
Number of blocks: 25

Setting: Five by five setting with three different blocks

Amount/Fabric	Piece/Amount	1st Cut	2nd Cut	Assembly
2 yds. – Sky background or very light print	**Inner Border**	(4) 1½" strips on lengthwise grain		
	House Blocks – Sky/roof units – 12	(3) 2" strips	Strip piecing	(See instructions)
	Mountain Blocks – Sky	(3) 3⅞" strips	(6) 3⅞" squares (Cut once diagonally)	
	Sky	(2) 3½" strips	(12) 3½" squares	
	Flying Geese units – 72	(5) 2⅜" strips	(72) 2⅜" squares	(FG – pg. 18)
	Trunk/sky units – 24	(4) 2⅛" strips		(See instructions)
	Schoolhouse Block Sky/roof unit – 1	(2) 2" x 4¼" rectangles (2) 3" squares		(See instructions)
	Belltower roof unit – 1	(2) 1¼" squares		(See instructions)
	Pieced Inner Border Checkerbd. units – 196	(8) 1½" strips	Strip piecing	(See instructions)
¼ yd. each – Three very dark prints	**Mountain Blocks – Tree Trunks** Trunk/sky units – 24	(1) 1" strip each fabric	Strip piecing	(See instructions)
	House Blocks – Roof Sky/roof units – 12	(1) 3" strip each fabric	Strip piecing	(See instructions)
	Schoolhouse Block – Roof Belltower roof unit – 1	(1) 1¼" x 2" rectangle		(See instructions)
	Sky/roof unit – 1	(1) 3" x 9½" rectangle		
¼ yd. each – Four medium prints	**House Blocks – Walls** Wall/window units – 24	(1) 2½" x 22" strip each fabric	Strip piecing	(See instructions)
	Walls – 48	(1) 4½" strip each fabric	(12) 1½" x 4½" rectangles each fabric	
¼ yd. each – Two medium/ dark prints	**House Blocks** Closed doors – 6	(1) 2" strip each fabric	(3) 2" x 4½" rectangles each fabric	
¼ yd. each – Four plaids	**House Blocks** Chimneys – 12	(1) 1½" strip each fabric	(3) 1½" x 8½" rectangles each fabric	
	Schoolhouse Block Walls	(1) 4½" strip (2) 4½" x 1½" rectangles (2) 2½" x 1¾" rectangles	(2) 4½" x 2" rectangles	
	Belltower wall	(1) 1¼" x 2" rectangle		
¼ yd. each – Two light, bright prints	**House Blocks** Window/wall units – 24	(1) 2½" x 22" strip each fabric	Strip piecing	(See instructions)
	Open doors – 6	(1) 2" strip each fabric	(3) 2" x 4½" rectangles each fabric	
	Schoolhouse Block Windows – 2	(2) 2½" x 1¾" rectangles		
	Open door – 1	(1) 2" x 4½" rectangle		
⅜ yd. each – Four med. dark prints	**House Blocks** Ground – 12	(1) 1½" strip each fabric	(3) 1½" x 9" rectangles each fabric	
	Mountain Blocks Ground – 12	(1) 9⅞" strip two fabrics	(3) 9⅞" squares each fabric (Cut once diagonally)	
	Schoolhouse Block Ground/step unit – 1	(2) 3½" x 1½" rectangles of one fabric (1) 3½" x 1½" rectangle of second fabric		
¼ yd. each (or scraps) – Six medium/dark greens	**Mountain Blocks** Flying Geese units – 72	(3) 4¼" squares each fabric or (18) 4¼" squares from scraps	(FG – pg. 18)	
⅜ yd. – Red plaid	**Inner Pieced Border** Checkerbd. units – 196	(7) 1½" strips	Strip piecing	(See instructions)
1⅝ yd. – Dark print/plaid 1 yd. – Dark 3⅞ yds. 64" x 64"	**Outer Border** **Binding** **Backing** **Batting**	(4) 5" strips on lengthwise grain (7) 2¾" strips on lengthwise grain Seam the width or length of the quilt		

The color and values of the doors and windows is what gives a different feeling to each house. Light, bright print windows give the house a lived-in look. A dark fabric door appears to be closed. When the door matches the windows, it appears to be open. In this quilt, each house and tree could be cut from different fabrics.

Barbara Dieges

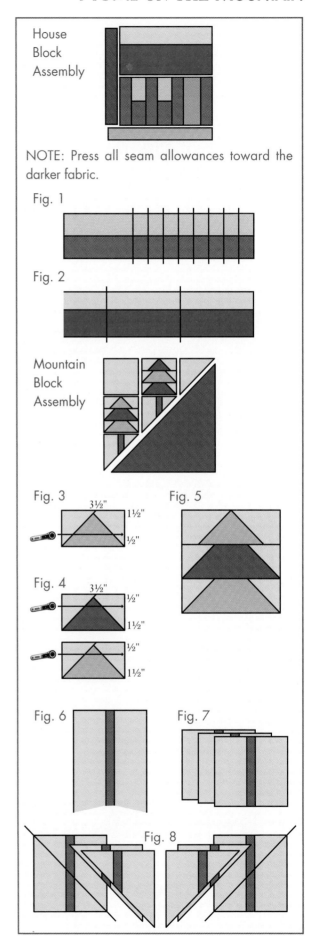

House Block Assembly

WINDOW/WALL UNITS (Fig. 1): Sew one 2½" x 22" window strip to a 2½" x 22" wall strip to make four window/wall bands. Cut six, 1¾" segments from each band.

SKY/ROOF UNITS (Fig. 2): Sew each 2" sky strip to a 3" roof strip to make three bands. Cut four, 8½" segments from each band.

Alternate four, 1½" x 4½" wall rectangles with two window/wall units and one, 2" x 4½" open or closed door rectangle (see House Block Assembly diagram). Add a sky/roof unit, a chimney rectangle, and a ground rectangle. For interest, vary the door and window placement as well as the chimney placement in the blocks.

Mountain Blocks

The instructions for making the branches of the trees in these blocks call for Flying Geese units. If you look closely at my quilt, you will see that instead of using Flying Geese units, I used half-square triangle units. This caused too much bulk with the seam down the center of each tree, so Flying Geese units are a much better choice.

TREES – FLYING GEESE UNITS: Use 2⅜" squares of sky and 4¼" squares of tree fabric to make these units following the instructions for Flying Geese units shown on pg. 18.

Trim each Flying Geese unit to 3½" x 1½" as follows:
(Fig. 3) Top unit: Cut ½" off the bottom of 24 Flying Geese units, retaining the point.

(Fig. 4) CENTER AND BOTTOM UNITS: Cut ½" off the top of 48 Flying Geese units.

(Fig. 5) Sew three units together to form each tree. Make 24 trees. Press seam allowances toward the top of the tree.

TREE TRUNK/SKY UNITS (Fig. 6): Make two bands by sewing a 1" trunk fabric strip between two, 2⅛" strips of sky fabric. Press seam allowances under the trunk. The bands must measure 4¼" wide so be sure you are sewing with a scant ¼" seam allowance.

(Fig. 7) Cut across the bands to make 12, 4¼" squares.

(Fig. 8) Cut six of the squares diagonally from top left to bottom right. Cut the other six squares from the top right to bottom left.

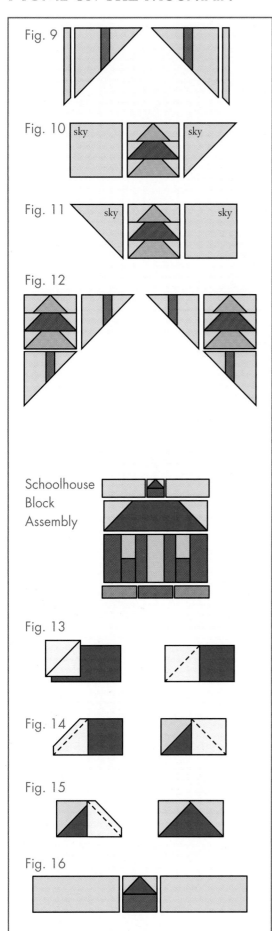

Fig. 9

Fig. 10

Fig. 11

Fig. 12

Schoolhouse Block Assembly

Fig. 13

Fig. 14

Fig. 15

Fig. 16

(Fig. 9) Trim ⅜" off the largest side of each triangle. Divide the trees into two groups of 12. One group of trees will be sewn onto a left-angled triangle; the other group will be sewn onto a right-angled triangle. Press seam allowances toward the trees.

(Fig. 10) Sew a 3½" sky square to the left side of six trees. Sew a 3⅞" sky triangle to the right side of the same units.

(Fig. 11) Sew a 3½" sky square to the right side of six trees. Sew a 3⅞" sky triangle to the left side of the same units.

(Fig. 12) Sew a trunk/sky triangle to the right side of six trees and sew a trunk/sky triangle to the bottom of the same six units. Sew a trunk/sky triangle to the left side of six trees, then sew a trunk/sky triangle to the bottom of the same six units.

Sew two right-angled tree units together and attach them to a right-angled mountain triangle (see Mountain Block assembly diagram, pg. 41). Make six right-angled mountain blocks. Repeat, making six left-angled mountain blocks.

Schoolhouse Block Assembly

BELLTOWER ROOF UNIT (Figs. 13 & 14): Align a 1¼" sky square with one end of the belltower roof rectangle. Draw a line diagonally across the square and sew on this line. Cut off the outside corner and press the sewn portion back. Repeat on the other end of the rectangle. (Fig. 15) The squares will overlap in the center.

(Fig. 16) Sew the belltower roof unit to the belltower wall rectangle. Then sew a 2" x 4¼" sky rectangle to either end.

SCHOOLHOUSE ROOF UNIT (Fig. 17): Align a 3" sky square with one end of the 3½" x 9½" schoolhouse roof rectangle. Draw a line diagonally across the square and sew on the line. Cut off the outside corner and press the sewn portion back. Repeat on the opposite end.

Sew the 2½" x 1¾" window rectangles together with the 2½" x 1¾" wall rectangles (see Schoolhouse Block assembly diagram).

Sew the "step" rectangle between the two ground rectangles and press the seam allowances under the step. Assemble the Schoolhouse Block as shown in the assembly diagram.

Quilt Assembly

Position the blocks as shown in the Quilt Assembly diagram.

Inner Border

After setting the blocks together, measure the height and width of the quilt top. It should measure 45½" x 45½" including seam allowances. From the 1½" lengthwise strips of sky fabric that you cut first, trim the inner border strips to your exact quilt top measurements. The extra pieces are used for the pieced inner border. Attach the side border strips first, then the top and bottom borders (see the Quilt Assembly diagram).

Pieced Inner Border

(Fig. 18) With right sides together, sew 1½" strips of sky and red plaid along the long edges. When you reach the end of a sky strip, lay another sky strip next to the first with edges touching and continue the seam. Do the same when a plaid strip runs out. Sew on piece after piece in this fashion.

Press the sewn strips open, and press the seam allowances toward the darker fabric. Cut into 196, 1½" segments, avoiding the strip seams as you cut. If more are needed, cut 1½" squares of sky fabric and sew to individual 1½" red plaid squares.

(Fig. 19) For the sides, make two pieced border strips with 47 segments each. Start with the dark fabric square on top and alternate the segments, ending with the dark square on the top. Sew the strips to the sides as shown. Rotate the pieced strips so the dark end squares are next to the quilt top.

(Fig. 20) Make two pieced border strips of 51 segments each for the top and bottom. Start the row by positioning a segment with the dark square at the bottom, then alternate the segments as you sew. End with a dark square on the bottom. Sew the strips to the top and bottom, rotating them so the dark end squares will be sewn to the quilt top. Abut the seam allowances of the side pieced strips (see the Quilt Assembly diagram).

Outer Border

Measure the height of your quilt top. Cut two 5" border strips to that measurement. Sew to the sides.

Measure the width of your quilt top and cut two, 5" border strips to that size. Sew to the top and bottom.

Quilting

This quilt is mostly quilted in the ditch with large stippling in the sky areas. Bears and trees are quilted in the borders.

Binding

Prepare a ⅜" binding according to directions on pg. 25.

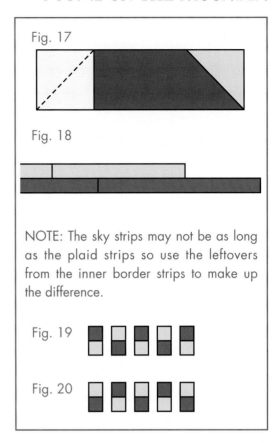

Fig. 17

Fig. 18

NOTE: The sky strips may not be as long as the plaid strips so use the leftovers from the inner border strips to make up the difference.

Fig. 19

Fig. 20

Quilt Assembly

KALEIDOSCOPE

"A blue quilt, Mama."

"But Rebecca, what about other colors?" I asked.

"No, all blue."

So I found many blue bits and pieces, even traded some with my neighbors and made this quilt top for Rebecca. There are pieces in there from some of her dresses and some from John's mother.

I decided on the KALEIDOSCOPE block. It fits her – she's always changing.

We all think of colors in different ways. I always thought navy was blue, but she said it was too dark. She was disappointed when I showed her the quilt top – said she didn't like it. Will she remember she said that, or is it only in my heart?

One of these days I'll quilt it. I just lost the delight in making it when she didn't like the colors. That is part of the parting. If I let go, she'll try her wings and fly back to me.

Barbara Dieges

Quilt top size:
47½" x 91"
Finished block size:
7¼"

Number of blocks:
55 with 28 edge
blocks
Setting: Five by
eleven blocks

Barbara Dieges

Amount/Fabric	Piece/Amount	1st Cut	2nd Cut
⅝ yd. – Very light print scraps, or four fat quarters – Light prints	**Background squares** – 72	(6) 3½" strips	(12) 3½" squares from each strip
	Triangles – 116 Template A	(4) 4½" strips each fabric	(8) 45° triangles each strip
Scraps, or 4 fat quarters – Medium prints/plaids	**Triangles** – 112 Template A	(4) 4½" strips each fabric	(8) 45° triangles each strip
Scraps or eight fat quarters – Dark prints/plaids	**Triangles** – 252 Template A	(4) 4½" strips each fabric	(8) 45° triangles each strip
¾ yd. – Light print	**Edge Block "Kites"** Template B Template Br	(6) 4" strips Left-angled "kites" – 28 Right-angled "kites" – 28	(10) "kite" shapes from each strip (Cut half right- and half left-angled)
1⅛ yds. – Medium print	**Border** Straight pieces Corner center Corner side (right) Template C Corner side (left)	(6) 2½" strips on lengthwise grain (4) 2¹¹⁄₁₆" x 3½" rectangles (4) make Template C from pattern (4) flip Template C to make Template Cr	
1 yd. or scraps – Dark	**Binding**	2¾" bias strips	
5½ yds.	**Backing**	Seam the length of the quilt	
51" x 95"	**Batting**		

This quilt can have many different fabrics and can be made using scraps or by purchasing the amounts shown on the chart.

Cutting and marking pieces

Kaleidoscope has several odd-shaped patches that cannot be cut with conventional rotary methods. You may find it easier to make templates for those pieces. Templates are on pg. 49.

Because of the seams that meet in the centers of the blocks, and the inset seams necessary to connect the background squares, many quilters may find it easier to assemble this quilt using hand-piecing methods. Or use the machine for the straight seams and inset the squares by hand.

(Fig. 1) The 3½" background squares connecting the rows can be rotary cut, but for ease of construction, the corners of the finished seams on both triangles and squares should be marked prior to assembly.

(Fig. 2) A cardboard or plastic marking template will help speed the process. Use a large needle to punch small holes where the small dots appear on the template pieces. The hole must be large enough to accommodate a pencil tip or fine point pen.

Fig. 1
mark corners

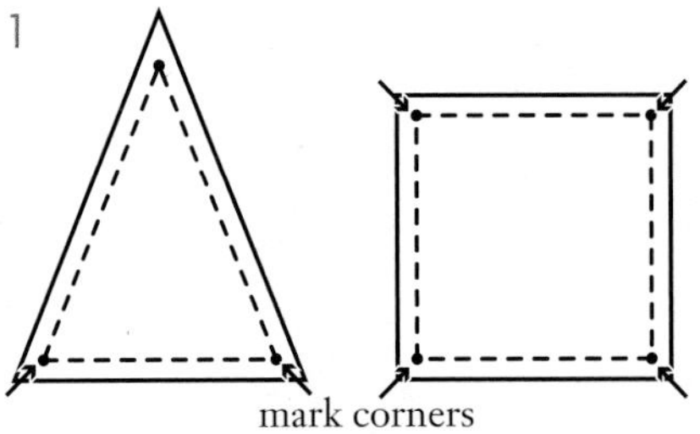

Fig. 2

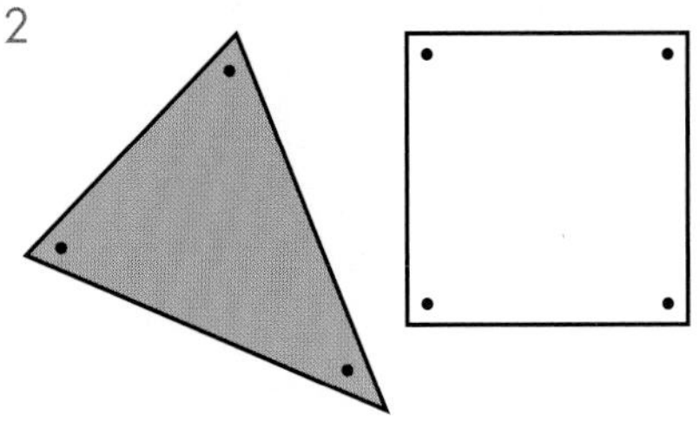

Mark the dots on the back of the fabric. Also mark the corners of the border block "kites" as shown on the template.

Block Assembly

Each block has four dark triangles that alternate with medium or light triangles. There are 28 blocks alternating dark with medium triangles and 27 blocks alternating dark with light triangles.

(Fig. 3) Sew the triangles together into pairs, matching the dots on both triangles. Start sewing at the dot with a back-stitch then sew down the seam and off the point.

(Fig. 4) Press the seam allowances under the left patch when viewed from the front. Trim off the protrusions.

Sew two pairs together, again matching the dots. The seam allowances will abut each other. Press the new seam allowance to the left and trim off the protrusions. Sew the halves together, matching the dots and center seams. The seam allowances will abut each other (see the Block Assembly diagram).

(Fig. 5) Turn the block over. At the very center, use a heavy pin to pick out the threads of the vertical seam back to the center seam. Do not cut these little threads or you will run the risk of your block opening at the center.

Setting the blocks

(Fig. 6) Alternate three dark/medium blocks and two dark/light blocks. Since the dark triangles will be sewn together, avoid placing two triangles of the same fabric next to each other.

Sew the dark triangles together, matching and sewing between the dots. Make six rows with this arrangement.

(Fig. 7) Alternate three dark/light blocks and two dark/medium blocks. Make five rows with this arrangement.

Setting the rows

(Fig. 8) Follow the techniques on pg. 15 for sewing inset seams. Set in the four center 3½" background squares by matching the dots of the square and the dots on the light and medium triangles. Then sew the squares into the next row.

Sew the dark triangles together, matching and sewing between the dots. Repeat for the remaining rows. After all of the rows are sewn together, set in the outer background squares.

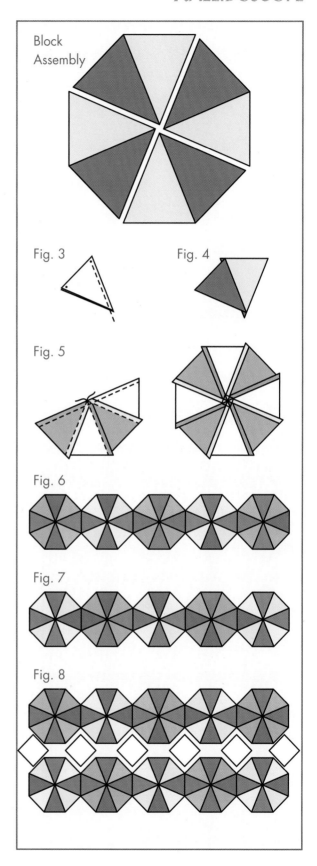

Block Assembly

Fig. 3

Fig. 4

Fig. 5

Fig. 6

Fig. 7

Fig. 8

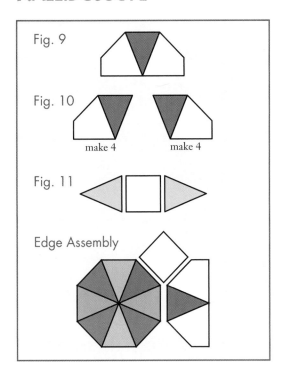

Fig. 9

Fig. 10

make 4   make 4

Fig. 11

Edge Assembly

Quilt Assembly

Edge blocks

(Fig. 9) Sew left- and right-angled "kite"-shaped patches on both sides of 24 dark triangles. Match and start sewing at the dots. Press seam allowances under the triangle. Make 24 units.

(Fig. 10) Make eight partial units for the ends of the edge blocks. Make four units with the triangle sewn on the left of the "kite" patch and four with the triangle sewn on the right of the "kite" patch.

(Fig. 11) For the corner units, sew a 3½" background square between two light triangles. Make four of these units.

Attach the edge block rows by setting in the squares (see the Quilt Assembly diagram). Then sew the dark triangles together, matching and sewing between the dots. Finish the seams between the edge blocks. Set in the corner units as shown in the Quilt Assembly diagram.

Border

Measure the straight edges of the quilt top from the point of the first dark triangle to the point of the last triangle (see the Quilt Assembly diagram). The short edges should measure 29". Add ½" to your measurement for seam allowances and cut two strips to that length.

Sew the remaining four border strips into pairs. Measure the long edges of the quilt top (see the Quilt Assembly diagram); they should measure 72½". Add ½" to your measurement for seam allowances and cut each sewn pair to that length.

Make four border corner units by sewing a border corner center between two border corner side pieces. Sew the border strips to the corner units to make a continuous piece (see the Quilt Assembly diagram). Sew the border to the quilt top matching the corner unit seams with the dark triangle points.

Quilting

Kaleidoscope remains unfinished to this day, awaiting the time when a daughter's disappointment turns to acceptance and fuels the desire to finish the quilt. When that day comes, an overall quilting pattern of shells or fans would be a nice choice for this quilt top.

Binding

Since this quilt has curved edges, it will have a finished ⅜" bias binding. Cut 8 yards of 2¾" bias strips from a dark fabric or cut bias strips from the different fabrics in the quilt. See pg. 25 for binding information.

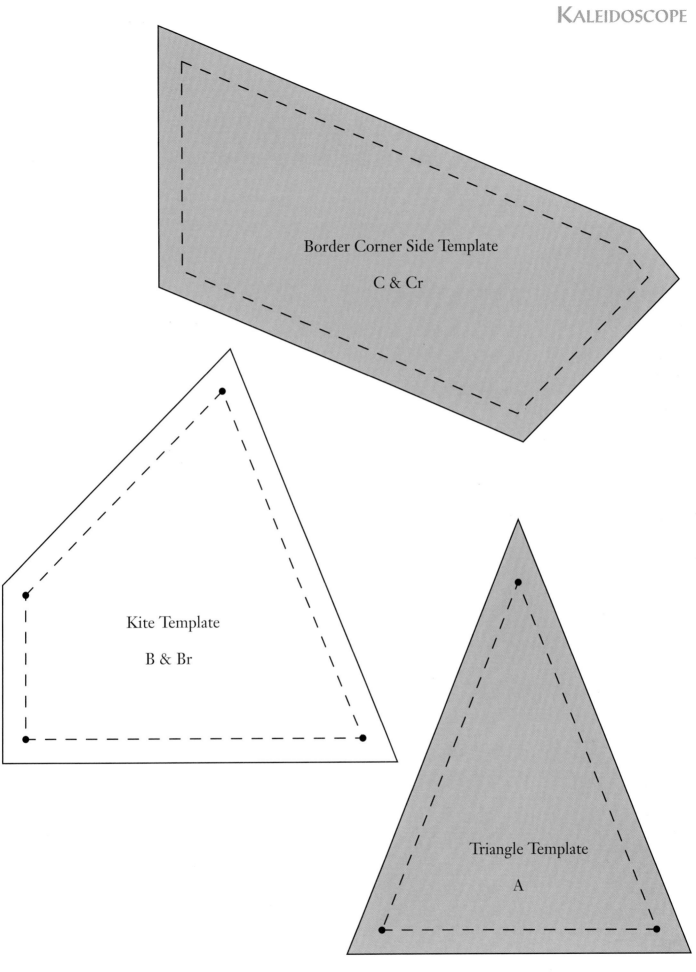

Border Corner Side Template

C & Cr

Kite Template

B & Br

Triangle Template

A

Barbara Dieges

WHEELS GOING across the PRAIRIE

This quilt was long in the making.

That pink lily vine grew in Sarah's garden. I admired it, so she gave me a cutting. Now that same vine is scrambling all over the porch roof.

We grew up together and told each other secrets. She was my best friend. I still use her apple pie recipe – she made it with maple syrup.

I remember when Sarah moved away. She married and when their children were young, they moved to the Oregon Territory. My, some of the things she saw going cross country in a covered wagon. Those stars made me think of WHEELS GOING ACROSS THE PRAIRIE.

She wrote letters about the trip and the hardships. I kept those letters and still read them sometimes.

Their son was so sick he almost died, but they got him through it. Other children did die and they buried them along the trail. Those mothers left little pieces of their hearts buried with them.

Sarah's children are all grown now. I'll probably never see her again. We'd be old and wouldn't know each other.

Barbara Dieges

Finished size: 88" x 96"
Finished block size: 33⁵⁄₁₆"
Number of blocks: 4

Setting: Two by two with sashing

Barbara Dieges

Amount/Fabric	Piece/Amount	1st Cut	2nd Cut	Assembly
1 yd. – Pink print	**Blocks**			(See pg. 15)
	Garland diamonds	(4) 2½" strips	(32) 2½" 45° diamonds	(See instructions)
	Center star diamonds	(10) 2⅛" x 28" strips		(FG – pg. 18)
	Border – Flying Geese	(6) 5¼" squares		
	Appliqué – Blooms			
	Back petals	(108) Template 1 – pg. 56		
½ yd. – Second pink print	**Blocks**			
	Center star diamonds	(4) 2⅛" x 28" strips		(See instructions)
	Appliqué – Blooms			
	Left front petals	(36) Template 5 – pg. 56		
	Right front petals	(36) Template 6 – pg. 56		
1 yd. – Orange print or solid	**Blocks**			
	Garland diamonds	(7) 2½" strips	(64) 2½" 45° diamonds	
	Center star diamonds	(2) 2⅛" x 28" strips		(See instructions)
	Border – Flying Geese	(6) 5¼" squares		(FG – pg. 18)
	Appliqué – Blooms			
	Flower Centers	(36) Template 2 – pg. 56		
2 yds. – Dark green solid	***Appliqué – Vines**	(11) 1" bias strips		
	Blocks			
	Garland diamonds	(4) 2½" strips	(32) 2½" 45° diamonds	
	Center star diamonds	(12) 2⅛" x 28" strips		(See instructions)
	Border – Flying Geese	(5) 5¼" squares		(FG – pg. 18)
½ yd. – Dark green print	**Blocks**			
	Garland diamonds	(4) 2½" strips	(32) 2½" 45° diamonds	(See instructions)
	Appliqué – Blooms			
	Calyx	(36) Template 4 (pg. 56) from each fabric		
3 fat quarters – Dark green prints	**Appliqué – Leaves**	(38) Template 3 (pg. 56) from each fabric		
¾ yd. – Red print or solid	**Blocks**			
	Center star diamonds	(8) 2⅛" x 28" strips		(See instructions)
	Border – Flying Geese	(5) 5¼" squares		(FG – pg. 18)
4 yds. – White on white or very light tiny print or muslin	****Appliqué – background**			
	Appliqué borders	(1) 7" strip on lengthwise grain		
	Corners	(2) 11" squares		(See instructions)
	Sashing rectangles	(4) 5" x 15" strips		
	Center block	(1) 25" square		
	Side appliqué pieces	(4) 11" x 26" rectangles		
	Blocks – background			
	Triangle	(4) 11" squares	Twice diagonally	
	Triangle	(8) 7¹³⁄₁₆" squares	Once diagonally	
	Garland triangle (qs)	(12) 5⁵⁄₁₆" squares	Twice diagonally	
	Garland triangle (hs)	(24) 3¾" squares	Once diagonally	
	Garland rectangle	(32) 3⅜" x 6¼" rectangles		
3 yds. – Light/medium varicolored print	**Inner borders**	(2) 6" strips on lengthwise grain		
	Blocks			
	Center star diamonds	(8) 2⅛" x 28" strips		(See instructions)
	Border – Flying Geese	(88) 2⅞" squares		(FG – pg. 18)
2½ yds. – Red print or solid	**Outer border**	(4) 3½" strips on lengthwise grain		
	Binding	(5) 3½" strips on lengthwise grain		
6 yds.	**Backing**	(2) 3 yard lengths		
1 yd.	**Backing strip**	(3) 12" x 36" strips on lengthwise grain	Sew into one long strip	
1 pkg. – Freezer paper	**Appliqué**	(112) Template 1 – pg. 56		
		(36) Template 2 – pg. 56		
		(112) Template 3 – pg. 56		
		(36) Template 4 – pg. 56		
92" x 100"	**Batting**			

* Appliqué – Vines – Cut bias strips for appliqué vines before cutting other pieces. Each strip is about 60 inches long. Piecing is not necessary. After cutting the bias strips, large triangles of fabric remain from both ends of the yardage. Use these fabric triangles for the star patches.

** Background – Cut the large pieces needed for the borders, center, and corner appliqué before cutting star patches. The appliqué patches are cut larger than needed to allow for fraying during handling. When the appliqué is finished and pressed, trim to the sizes needed.

Block Assembly

CENTER STAR DIAMONDS

The small diamonds in the center stars are not sewn individually but are made of strips of six fabrics, sewn together into bands, then cut into segments. The segments are sewn together to form the larger diamond units. Two sets each of four diamond units, right pointing and left pointing, are needed for each star.

RIGHT POINTING DIAMOND UNITS (Fig. 1)

(Fig. 2) Sew together the 2⅛" x 28" strips for bands 1, 2, and 3, making two strips sets for each band. The strips are offset about 1½", stair-stepped to the right to lessen the amount of waste when the segments are cut. Press the seam allowances of bands 1 and 3 down and the seam allowances of band 2 up.

(Fig. 3) Align the 45° line on a rotary ruler with a seam line, positioning the ruler so the offsets will be completely removed; trim off the offset edge.

(Fig. 4) Rotate the band so the diagonal edge is on the left. Align the ruler on a seam and at 2⅛" then cut on the 45° diagonal. Cut 8, 2⅛" segments from each band for a total of 16. Mark each set to keep them separate.

(Fig. 5) Layout a segment from each of the three bands. Match the seam lines so they abut and the points of the segments protrude. Make 16 right pointing diamond units.

LEFT POINTING DIAMOND UNITS (Fig. 6)

The same basic steps are repeated when assembling the left pointing diamonds.

(Fig. 7) For these units the bands are offset 1½" to the left. Sew the strips together to form the bands. Press the seam allowances of bands 4 and 6 up and the seam allowances of band 5 down.

(Fig. 8) Repeat the steps for assembling the left facing diamonds, but remember to position the ruler in the opposite direction when cutting. Make 16 left pointing diamond units.

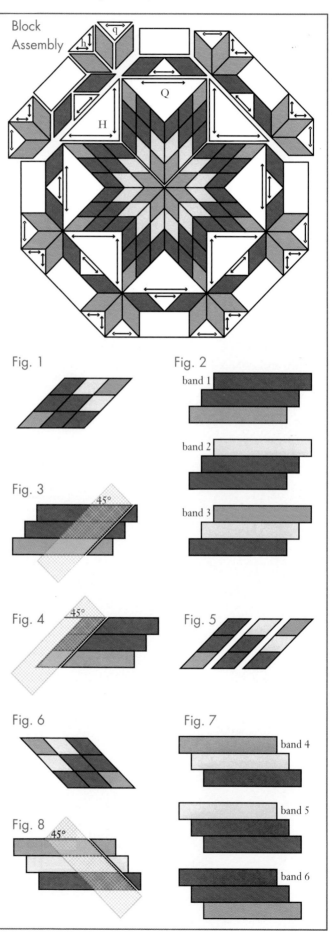

Block Assembly

Fig. 1

Fig. 2

band 1

band 2

band 3

Fig. 3

45°

Fig. 4 45°

Fig. 5

Fig. 6

Fig. 7

band 4

band 5

Fig. 8 45°

band 6

Background Triangles

The background triangles used to complete the center stars are the same sizes, but were cut differently and have different grainlines. I would recommend identifying these triangles as (Q) and (H) for ease when assembling. The longest edge of the (Q) triangles inset first between two left and right pointing diamond units is on the straight of grain. The (H) triangles inset after the diamond units are assembled together have a bias grainline on the longest edge. When assembling the blocks, watch the positioning of the triangles very carefully. The straight of grain for the triangles is also indicated on the Block Assembly diagram by arrows.

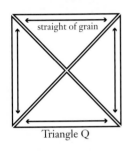

Triangle Q

Triangle H

Fig. 10

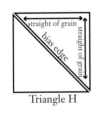

Fig. 11

Fig. 12

Fig. 13

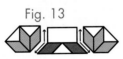

Fig. 14

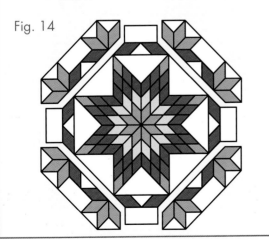

Center Star Assembly

Mark the center pieced diamond units and the (Q) and (H) triangles (see pg. 15 for information on Y-seams).

Sew a pair of right facing and left facing diamond units together and inset a (Q) triangle (see Background Triangles at left). Make four diamond and triangle units for each block. Connect the units together (see the Block Assembly diagram), starting at the marked points. If you pressed the seam allowances correctly, the center seams will abut each other. Match the center seam carefully before sewing across it.

(Fig. 10) Set in the (H) triangles (see Background Triangles at left).

Garland Assembly

Mark the seam intersections on the garland diamonds, garland rectangles, and (q) and (h) garland triangles.

(Fig. 11) Make four units with a (q) garland triangle between two green garland diamonds. Sew a garland rectangle to the top of this unit. Make four. Sew these units to the (Q) triangles of the center star (Block Assembly diagram).

Make four similar units, this time using an (h) garland triangle between two garland diamonds. Sew a garland rectangle to the top as in Figure 11. Set aside.

(Fig. 12) Using the Y-seam technique, make eight diamond/triangle units from two orange garland diamonds, one pink garland diamond and one (h) and one (q) garland triangle.

(Fig. 13) Make four garland units by sewing each of the units set aside earlier between two diamond/triangle units. Sew the seam between the rectangle and the diamond first, then between the two diamonds.

(Fig. 14) Sew the garland units to the center star, using the same sewing techniques as above. Match seam intersections. Sew the short seams first, then the long seam. Make all four stars in the same manner.

Appliqué

To help place appliqué pieces on the background fabric, lightly mark lines showing the trimming size (includes seam allowance) along the edges of the background fabric.

Stop vine and flower appliqué 1" from the marked lines.

Before trimming the appliqué pieces, pin loose vines out of the way.

BORDERS: Follow the schematics on pgs. 56 and 57 for guidance in positioning appliqué pieces. Trim the border pieces to the sizes indicated on the Quilt Assembly diagram after appliquéing.

CORNERS: Appliqué two opposite corners of two 11" squares, top right and bottom left. Cut the squares in half diagonally between the flowers then trim the pieces to size.

SIDE APPLIQUÉ: After appliquéing, trim the rectangles to the size shown on the Quilt Assembly diagram. Align the 45° line on a rotary ruler with the top edge and corner of the rectangle. Cut the corners diagonally to achieve the shape shown.

CENTER: Trim the 25" square to 24⅜" as indicated in the Quilt Assembly diagram. Cut a plastic or paper template 9⅞" square. Cut in half diagonally. Align a triangle with one corner of the fabric square and cut off the corner along the diagonal edge of the triangle template. Repeat with the other three corners.

Quilt Top Assembly
With the exception of the border strips, trim all of the appliqué pieces to the sizes on the Quilt Assembly diagram. Mark seam intersections on the appliqué pieces. Sew the appliqué triangles and rectangles to the stars as shown in the Quilt Assembly diagram.

Set in the center between the diagonally opposite stars. Set in the remaining two stars, finishing the seams between the appliqué rectangles and then the center side appliqué.

Measure the width of the quilt top, it should measure 71½". Cut the appliqué borders to that length. Do not trim the width of the border strips until after measuring the height of the quilt.

Measure the height of the quilt top. It should measure 71½" including seam allowances. The minimum unfinished width of the border strips is 6" (5½" after finishing), giving an overall finished height of 82".

Attach the appliqué borders to the top and bottom of the quilt top. Finish the vine and leaf appliqué where the vines travel across the seams.

NOTE: It is important that the finished height of the quilt top be an amount divisible by 2 so the Flying Geese border will fit along the sides. So, if necessary trim the long edges of the appliqué borders at the top and bottom.

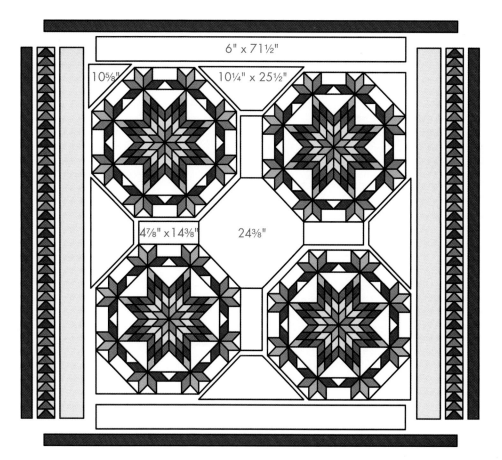

Quilt Assembly
The appliqué patches are illustrated without the appliqué to more clearly show positioning.

Barbara Dieges

Inner side borders

Measure the height of the quilt top, it should measure 82½", including seam allowances. Cut the two light/medium varicolored print border strips to that measurement. Sew to the sides.

Flying Geese side borders

If the height of the quilt measures 82½", make 88 Flying Geese units. Using the fast technique for making Flying Geese (pg. 18), you will end up with more Flying Geese units than necessary.

Sew the Flying Geese patches into two rows of 41 each. (This is slightly different than the quilt photo.) Pin to both sides of the quilt top being careful to pin evenly. Sew in place.

Outer border

Measure the width of the quilt top. It should measure 90½". Trim two of the strips to this measurement. Pin and sew to the top and bottom of the quilt top.

Measure the height of the quilt top. It should now measure 88½". Trim the remaining two strips to this length. Pin and sew to the sides of the quilt top.

Backing

Sew a 12" backing strip between two, 3 yard lengths.

Quilting

Cross-hatch quilting at 2" intervals is in the background. The diamonds are outlined in the ditch and stitched in the center in both directions. The borders have undulating designs with the Flying Geese quilted in the ditch.

Binding

This quilt has a finished ½" binding cut from the same fabric as the border. See pg. 25 for information on binding.

After ironing the fabric to the paper, whipstitch the edges together where the petals touch. It is easier to appliqué this as a unit than one petal at a time. The paper can be pulled out at the bottom before the flower center is added.

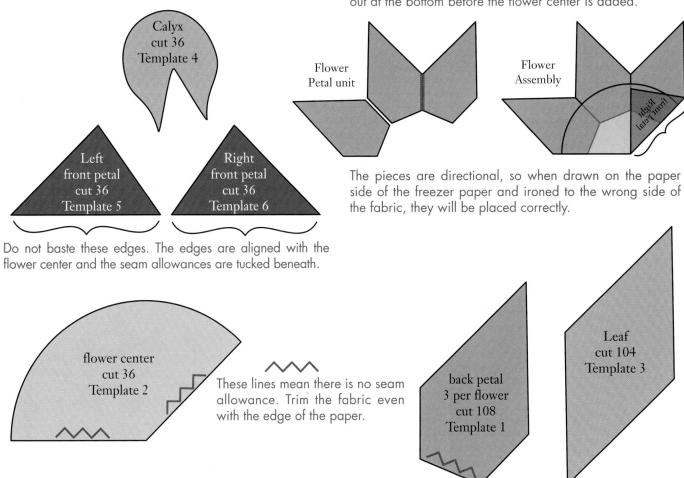

Calyx
cut 36
Template 4

Flower
Petal unit

Flower
Assembly

Right
front petal

Left
front petal
cut 36
Template 5

Right
front petal
cut 36
Template 6

Do not baste these edges. The edges are aligned with the flower center and the seam allowances are tucked beneath.

The pieces are directional, so when drawn on the paper side of the freezer paper and ironed to the wrong side of the fabric, they will be placed correctly.

flower center
cut 36
Template 2

These lines mean there is no seam allowance. Trim the fabric even with the edge of the paper.

back petal
3 per flower
cut 108
Template 1

Leaf
cut 104
Template 3

Border Appliqué Assembly

center

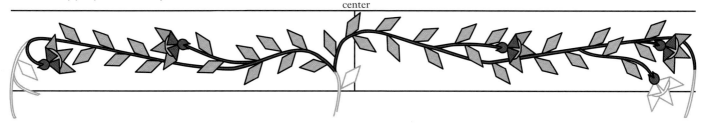

Center Appliqué Assembly

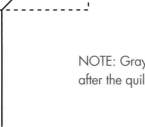

Side Appliqué Assembly

Corner Appliqué Assembly

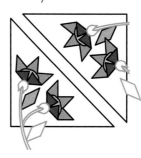

NOTE: Grayed appliqué is finished after the quilt tip is assembled.

Appliqué Assembly

Barbara Dieges

A Thread *runs* through it

ANGLES 'n SQUARES

Some important folks wrote to John. They had heard about his work and wanted his help with a church they were building in the city. We thought about it long and hard. The money would help, so he went, but he came home when his part of the work was slow.

Most times folks here didn't think much about fine furniture or cabinets. They would make do with what they had or put something together themselves. Sometimes John got paid to build a house or barn. Mostly neighbor folks did barn-raisings, when all helped together.

We have our land, so we have something – something to build on and grow. We've made do. He'd have more work in the city, but here on the mountain we have more life.

Life and piecing go hand in hand. You're given a bunch of bits and pieces. How you put them all together makes the difference.

I worked on Angles 'n' Squares when John was away. Those were times when it was hard. I was alone here with the children, taking care of the animals and garden. Didn't have much time, but here a little, there a little, and it came together. Mama would come and help, but she could only stay so long. When Mama was here we were really quilting just to finish those quilts.

We made other quilts with old work clothes and heavy wools. They weren't quilted, just tied. Each patch was different, just as we all are different. It all works together, and so can we.

It took a lot of covers to keep a family warm. In the winter you'd want a heavy quilt, even a bunch. You could barely turn over under all those quilts. Somehow it just felt warmer when you were held in place and couldn't move.

Barbara Dieges

Finished size: 57" x 73"
Finished block size: 8"
Number of blocks: 48

Setting: Six by eight blocks
Layout variations shown on pg. 62.

Barbara Dieges

ANGLES 'N SQUARES

This quilt uses all print and plaid fabrics. Fabric and cutting instructions for two variations of this quilt are given here. The coordinated quilt block version uses the same three light and three dark fabrics in all blocks. The scrappy version uses 14 different fabrics in each block. You could also make this quilt as a charm quilt in which none of the fabrics are repeated. To make all 48 blocks would require 672 different fabric pieces. The smallest piece you would need is 2½", the largest is 4½".

Whichever version you decide to make, contrast is very important. The lights should be as light as possible. White or off-white prints, or tiny prints on white, or off-white, are good choices. The dark prints can be anything from mediums to very dark prints in any color or size of print.

Amount/Fabric	Piece/Amount	1st Cut	2nd Cut	Assembly
Coordinated Quilt Blocks				
⅜ yd. – #1 Light	Half–square triangles	(4) 5¾" strips	(24) 5¾" squares	(HSTM – pg. 18)
⅜ yd. – #1 Dark	Half–square triangles	(4) 5¾" strips	(24) 5¾" squares	(HSTM – pg. 18)
⅞ yd. – #2 Light	Large squares	(6) 4½" strips	(48) 4½" squares	
⅞ yd. – #2 Dark	Large squares	(6) 4½" strips	(48) 4½" squares	
½ yd. – #3 Light	Small squares	(6) 2½" strips	(96) 2½" squares	
½ yd. – #3 Dark	Small squares	(6) 2½" strips	(96) 2½" squares	
Variation – Scrappy Fat Quarter Blocks (each block has 14 different fabrics)				
There are 14 fabrics in each block and when the strips are cut and sewn for the half–square triangles, there will be extras. There are also extras of each of the other squares. This gives you more choices when arranging the fabrics within each block.				
7 fat quarters – Lights	**Blocks**			
	Half–square triangles	(2) 5¾" squares from each fabric		(HSTM – pg. 18)
	Large squares	(7) 4½" squares from each fabric		
	Small squares	(14) 2½" squares from each fabric		
7 fat quarters – Darks	**Blocks**			
	Half–square triangles	(2) 5¾" squares from each fabric		(HSTM – pg. 18)
	Large squares	(7) 4½" squares from each fabric		
	Small squares	(14) 2½" squares from each fabric		
1⅞ yd. – Medium print	**Inner Border**	(4) 2" strips on lengthwise grain		
2 yds. – Dark print or plaid	**Outer Border**	(4) 3¼" strips on lengthwise grain		
1 yd. – Dark print	**Binding**	(8) 2¾" strips on lengthwise grain		
4½ yds.	**Backing**	Seam the length of the quilt		
61" x 77"	**Batting**			

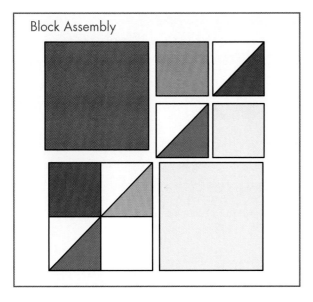

Block Assembly

Assembling the Units

HALF-SQUARE TRIANGLES: Using 5¾" squares of lights and darks, make four half-square triangles for each block following the multiples method on pg. 18.

FOUR-PATCH ASSEMBLY: Separate the light and dark 2½" squares into two stacks. For a scrappy quilt, make sure the squares are well mixed since pieces of the same fabrics should not appear in the same block.

Separate the half-square triangles into two stacks, making sure that the light triangle is always at the bottom left.

(Fig. 1) Set four stacks of patches to the left of the sewing machine, positioned exactly as shown.

   Dark square / half-square triangle
   Half-square triangle / light square

(Fig. 2) Chain stitch the patches together, alternating sewing the pairs with light and dark squares together as you sew. Do not lift the presser foot between the patches and do not snip the threads between units until all of the units are sewn.

(Fig. 3) Cut apart in pairs, always making sure the dark square is at the top left, and the light square is at the bottom right with the diagonal line always aligned the same way.

(Fig. 4) Leave the pairs hooked together and sew the pairs into Four-Patch units.

Block Assembly
Separate the light and dark 4½" squares into two separate stacks. Make sure that the squares are well mixed so that two of the same fabric aren't stacked together.

(Fig. 5) Position squares and Four-Patch units exactly as shown.

   Dark square / Four-Patch unit
   Four-Patch unit / light square

(Fig. 6) Using the same chain stitching techniques as when sewing the Four-Patch, sew a dark 4½" square to a Four-Patch unit so that it is sewn on the same side as the 2½" dark square. Then, without lifting the presser foot, sew a light 4½" square to a Four-Patch so that it is sewn on the same side as the 2½" light square.

(Fig. 7) Do not cut the units apart. Continue sewing alternating pairs together. When all units are sewn, cut them apart in pairs and sew those two units together. Watch the alignment of the diagonal line.

Block Setting Variations
The blocks can be set together in a myriad of ways. Two additional possibilities are shown on pg. 62, but basically, any setting that is appropriate for Log Cabin blocks could also be used for ANGLES 'N SQUARES.

Play with the block arrangement before sewing the blocks together. Place them so they all face the same way. Try giving every other one a quarter turn. Play with other arrangements.

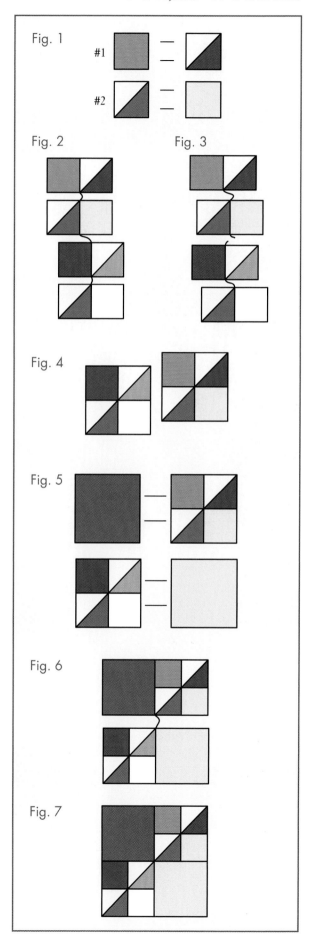

Block setting variations

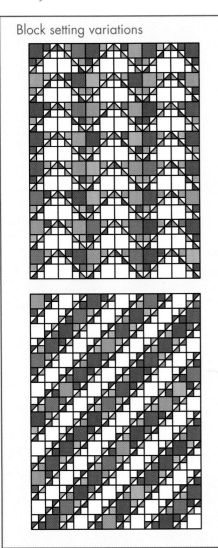

Borders

INNER BORDER: Measure the height of the quilt top, including seam allowances. It should measure 64½". Trim two of the 2" inner border strips to your measurement. Pin and sew to the sides of the quilt top.

Measure the width of the quilt top including the borders and seam allowances. It should measure 51½". Cut the remaining two strips to your measurement. Pin and sew to the top and bottom.

OUTER BORDER: Measure the height of the quilt top, including borders and seam allowances. It should measure 67½". Trim two 3¼" outer border pieces to your measurement. Pin and sew to the sides.

Measure the width of the quilt top including the borders and seam allowances. It should measure 57". Cut the remaining two strips to your measurement. Pin and sew to the top and bottom.

Quilting
Straight lines and a cable design are quilted following the dark and light areas of the quilt.

Binding
The quilt is bound with a ⅜" binding. (See pg. 25 for information on bindings.)

Quilt Assembly

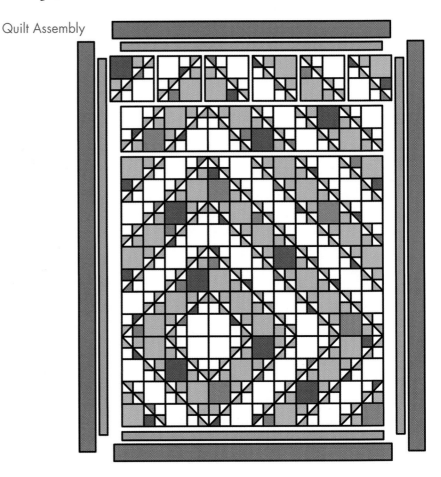

ETHAN'S QUILT

This is ETHAN'S QUILT. He always watched me when I was drawing my blocks, so he made this one. His mind worked like that. The more complicated a puzzle or problem, the more he enjoyed it.

I told him this pattern was harder than what I usually made, but that I'd figure it out, and sooner or later it would get done.

There he was, raised in the mountains, but he dreamt of the sea. Didn't talk much about it, but there was his dream.

He once wrote in a school paper about our mountains: "Imagination is not broad enough to claim the mountains of one's hopes, after all, mountains are only piles of men's dreams."

So the mountains must have been part of him after all.

Then he came home from the city one day and told us he had signed on a naval ship. He'd be leaving in two months to go to sea. Those months went fast, then he was gone. I fretted and worried. It was so long before we heard from him. Then when we did, the worrying was gone. He was fine and happy with his choice.

It was a long time before we saw him again.

Barbara Dieges

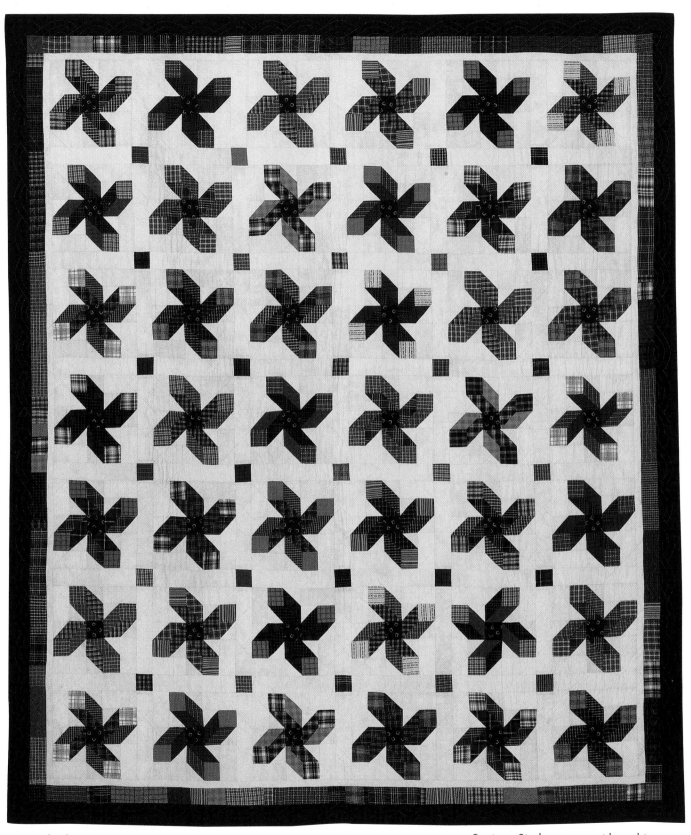

Finished size: 70¾" x 81¾"

Setting: Six by seven with sashing

Finished block size: 8¾"

Number of blocks: 42

There are 42 different plaids in this quilt – 14 light, 14 medium, and 14 dark. Each block needs three different plaids and the same three plaids appear in three blocks. When the blocks are placed randomly, it appears that the plaids are all different. The three values of plaid within each block should be different enough from each other to be distinguishable. The light value needs to be darker than the background but lighter than the other two fabrics.

Lesser amounts of fabric could be used to make this quilt. If you made six identical blocks in seven variations you would only need 21 plaids to make 42 blocks. The fabric and cutting requirements are provided for this option.

Amount/Fabric	Piece/Amount	1st Cut	2nd Cut
4¼ yds. – White print or muslin	**Inner border**	(1) 1½" strip the length of the fabric	
	Sashing	(18) 2¼" strips	(71) 2¼" x 9¼" rectangles
	Blocks		
	Rectangles	(19) 2¼" strips	(168) 2¼" x 4" rectangles
	Triangles – 336	(12) 2⅝" strips	(168) 2⅝" squares (cut once diagonally)
¼ yd. – Very dark or black	**Blocks – Center squares**	(3) 2¼" strips	(42) 2¼" squares
14 fat eighths* – Lt. plaids	**Blocks**		
	Outer squares – 210	(2) 2¼" strips each fabric	(15) 2¼" squares each fabric
	Sashing squares and border corners	(The extra 42 squares from above are used for the sashing squares, pieced border, and the corners.)	

Cut the following medium and dark pieces simultaneously by layering one dark and one medium with right sides together. Press them to help make the fabrics cling together. See pattern instructions for specific cutting directions. Do not separate pieces after cutting.

Amount/Fabric	Piece/Amount	1st Cut	2nd Cut
14 fat eighths* – Medium plaids	**Blocks**		
	Parallelograms – 168	(1) 2¼" strip each fabric	(12) 45° parallelograms each fabric
14 fat eighths* – Dark plaids	**Blocks**		
	Parallelograms – 168	(1) 2¼" strip each fabric	(12) 45° parallelograms each fabric
	Pieced Border	(Save extra medium and dark fabrics to use in cutting 2¼" wide pieces for the pieced border.)	
2¼ yds. – Dark print	**Outer border**	(4) 2¼" strips the length of the fabric	
	Binding	(4) 2¾" strips the length of the fabric	
5 yds.	**Backing**	(Seam the length of the quilt)	
75" x 86"	**Batting**		

* If you elect to make your quilt using all 42 plaids, try to purchase fat eighths (9" x 22") which will provide ample fabric for the blocks, sashing squares, and the pieced inner border. If fat eighths aren't available, ⅛ yard (4½") will also yield enough fabric.

ALTERNATIVE 21 FABRIC QUILT

7 fat quarters – Lt. plaids	**Blocks**		
	Outer squares – 168	(4) 2¼" strips each fabric	(24) 2¼" squares each fabric
	Sashing squares and border corners	(Save the excess from the strips and cut for the sashing and pieced border corners.)	(34) 2¼" squares

Cut the following parallelogram pieces together as indicated above and in the instructions.

7 fat quarters – Med. plaids	**Blocks**		
	Parallelograms – 168	(2) 2¼" strips each fabric	(24) 45° parallelograms each fabric
7 fat quarters – Dk. plaids	**Blocks**		
	Parallelograms – 168	(2) 2¼" strips each fabric (Save extra medium and dark fabrics to use in cutting 2¼" wide pieces for the pieced border.)	(24) 45° parallelograms each fabric

Barbara Dieges

Note: The angled shapes in the blocks are often referred to as diamonds, but they are actually parallelograms since the sides are unequal. (See pg. 15 for information on cutting and sewing parallelograms.)

Fig. 1

Fig. 2

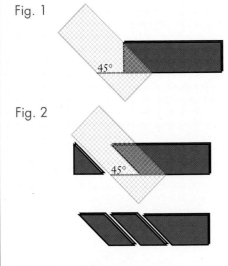

Block Assembly

Fig. 3

Fig. 4

Fig. 5

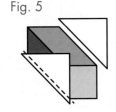

Fig. 6

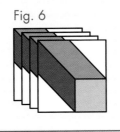

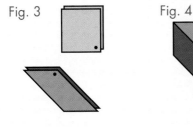

Cutting parallelograms

Cut the medium and dark fabrics simultaneously. Lay the medium fabric on top of the dark fabric, right sides together. Press with an iron to help the fabrics cling together. Do not separate the pieces after cutting.

(Fig. 1) Align the 45° line on the ruler with the long edge of the layered strips and the edge of the ruler with the left corner. Trim off the triangle at the edge and save it for another project.

(Fig. 2) Keep the ruler at the same angle and parallel to the diagonal cut. Move it over 1¾" and make another diagonal cut. Do not separate the pairs after cutting.

Repeat making diagonal cuts across the strips. Cut 12 sets of parallelograms from each fabric pair (24 if making the optional 21 fabric variation). Save the excess fabric to use for sashing squares and the pieced border.

Block Assembly

PARALLELOGRAM UNITS: See page 15, Diamonds, Parallelograms, and Y-seams, for marking, sewing, and setting in the squares. Instead of setting in a triangle, you will be setting in a square, but the same general principle applies.

(Fig. 3) To set in the light squares properly, all of the parallelograms and squares need to be marked at the seam intersections. Only one mark is necessary on each.

(Fig. 4) Sew the parallelogram seam, then inset the square. Each block requires four identical parallelogram/square units. Press the seam allowances toward the darkest fabric and trim off the protruding points.

(Fig. 5) Sew two background triangles to the parallelograms. The points of the triangles will protrude. Sew into and out of the "V," then press seam allowances toward the parallelograms.

SEWING THE BLOCK (Fig. 6): Stack the four parallelogram units for each block so the light plaid square is in the bottom right corner.

(Fig. 7) Sew a background rectangle across each right edge. Repeat for all the blocks, keeping the same fabric units together. Press seam allowances toward the darker fabric.

Barbara Dieges

(Fig. 8) Stack the four units for each block so that the rectangle is on the bottom. Align a dark center square with the corner formed by the parallelograms.

(Fig. 9) Sew a partial seam about halfway, stopping about 1" (arrow) from the bottom edge of the dark center square; backstitch. Fold the square out and finger press the seam allowance underneath the square.

(Fig. 10) Rotate the unit so the square is on the bottom. Align a diamond unit along the edge formed between the first diamond unit and the dark square and sew from the top down toward the dark square.

Continue, following the sewing sequence in Figure 10. Rotate the unit again and open the newly sewn unit. Sew a parallelogram unit along the edge formed between the second parallelogram unit and the square. Sew the last unit on in the same way then close the last seam by sewing from the outside of the block in to meet the partial seam. Press the blocks, making sure all of the seams are pressed toward the darkest fabrics.

Sashing

Sew five sashing rectangles between six pieced blocks to form a row; make seven rows (see the Quilt Assembly diagram). Press seam allowances toward the blocks.

Use 30 remaining 2¼" squares of light plaid fabrics and sew five squares between six sashing rectangles (see the Quilt Assembly diagram). Make six sashing/square rows. Press seam allowances under the squares. Sew the rows of blocks and sashing rows together.

Borders

INNER BORDER: Measure the height of the quilt top, including seam allowances. It should measure 72¼". From the 1½" x 4 yard background strip, cut two pieces to your measurement. Pin and sew to the sides.

Measure the width of the quilt top including borders and seam allowances. It should measure 63¾". From the remaining strip, cut two pieces to your measurement. Pin and sew to the top and bottom.

PIECED BORDER: Cut the remaining 2¼" strips of assorted plaid fabrics into squares and rectangles of different lengths. Sew these pieces together to make a strip 2¼" x 300", but avoid placing the same plaid next to, or close to, itself. The

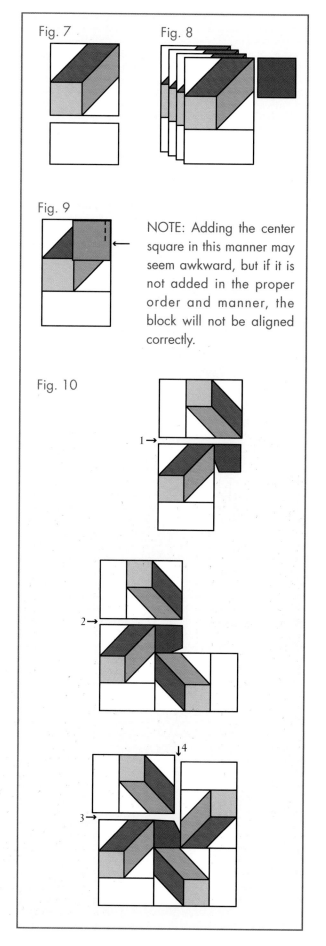

Fig. 7

Fig. 8

Fig. 9

NOTE: Adding the center square in this manner may seem awkward, but if it is not added in the proper order and manner, the block will not be aligned correctly.

Fig. 10

Barbara Dieges

300" length is longer than what is actually needed to allow leeway when cutting the strips for the border. Press all seam allowances in the same direction.

Measure the height and width of the quilt top. It should measure 63¾" x 74¼". Cut two strips of the sewn plaids to your height measurement, being careful not to cut too close to a seam. Pin and sew to the sides.

Cut the remaining strip into two 63¾" pieces. Sew one of the remaining four, 2¼" plaid squares to each end of the two strips. Align the end squares with the seams at edges of the quilt top. Pin and sew to the top and bottom of the quilt.

OUTER BORDER: Measure the height of the quilt top, including borders and seam allowances. It should measure 77¾". Cut two 2¼" strips to your measurement. Pin and sew to the sides.

Measure the width of the quilt top including the borders and seam allowances. It should measure 70¾". Cut the remaining two strips to your measurement. Pin and sew to the top and bottom.

Quilting

This quilt is quilted with an overall diagonal grid that follows the edges of the parallelograms. The quilting starts and stops at the corners of the sashing squares and when it reaches the patches. The border is quilted with a cable design large enough to cover both the pieced and outer borders.

Binding

This quilt has a finished ⅜" binding. (See pg. 25 for binding techniques.)

Quilt Assembly

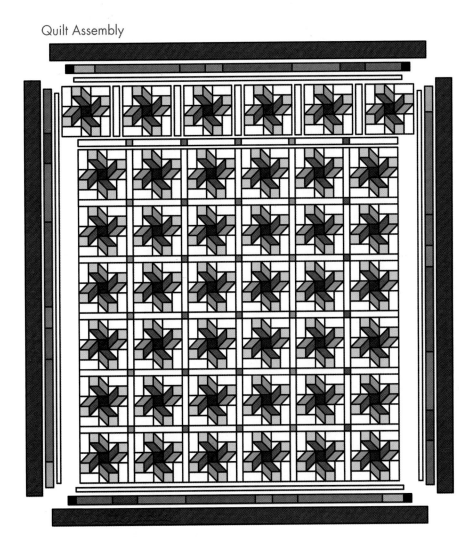

SAWTOOTH DIAMOND

This SAWTOOTH DIAMOND quilt came from my quilting granny, Papa's mother Minna. I never knew my other grandmother. Granny taught me all about stitching, quilting, and knitting.

My mama never seemed to enjoy quilting, but she did darning, mending, and sewing for necessity. I think in her heart she felt anything else was a waste of time. She loved gardening and baking. Those were the things she taught me.

She told me once that she would go to quilting bees, but she would rather be doing something else.

She kept after me though and didn't stop me from learning.

Barbara Dieges

Finished size: 71" x 71"
Number of blocks: 1

A Thread *runs* through it

Barbara Dieges

Amount/Fabric	Piece/Amount	1st Cut	2nd Cut	Assembly
3 yds. – Rust	**Half-square triangles**	(5) 4¾" strips (1) 4¾" square	(40) 4¾" squares (Cut from remaining fabric)	(HSTM – pg. 18)
	Center square	(1) 11" square		
	Large triangles	(2) 18⅞" squares	Once diagonally	
	Border	(4) 10¼" strips length of fabric		
3 yds. – Teal	**Half-square triangles**	(5) 4¾" strips (1) 4¾" square	(40) 4¾" squares (Cut from remaining fabric)	(HSTM – pg. 18)
	Inner border	(2) 5" strips (2) 5" x 23" rectangles	(2) 5" x 14" rectangles	
	Middle border	(2) 5" strips	(2) 5" x 39½" rectangles	
	Binding	(6) 5" strips length of fabric		
4½ yds.	**Backing**	Seam the length of the quilt		
75" x 75"	**Batting**			

Half-square Triangles

Layer the 41, 4¾" rust squares with the 41, 4¾" teal squares, right sides together. Make 328 half-square triangles following the instructions for multiple half-square triangles on pg. 18.

Follow the illustrations carefully to make the units for each round of half-square triangles. Be careful to follow the alignment and number of half-square triangles in each unit.

(Fig. 1) Make four round 1 units as shown:
Two with seven HST, and two with nine HST.

(Fig. 2) Make four round 2 units as shown:
Two with 15 HST, and two with 17 HST.

(Fig. 3) Make four round 3 units as shown:
Two with 24 HST, and two with 26 HST.

(Fig. 4) Make four round 4 units as shown:
Two with 32 HST, and two with 34 HST.

Quilt Assembly

ROUND 1 (Fig. 5): Sew two units with seven half-square triangles units to opposite sides of the 11" center square. Make certain the rust portion of the half-square triangles are next to the square. Press seam allowances toward the square.

Sew the two units with nine half-square triangles to the top and bottom of the square as shown in the Quilt Assembly diagram. Press seam allowances toward the square.

Inner Border

Pin and sew the 5" x 14" teal rectangles to the sides of the center square. Pin and sew the 5" x 23" teal rectangles to the top and bottom.

ROUND 2: Sew the two units with 15 half-square triangles to the sides of the center square. Rotate the units so the teal half-square triangles are sewn against the strips. Press seam allowances toward the strips.

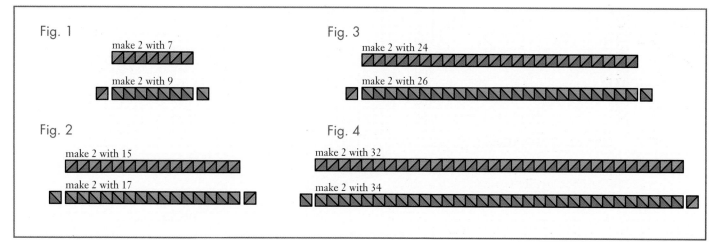

Fig. 1
make 2 with 7
make 2 with 9

Fig. 2
make 2 with 15
make 2 with 17

Fig. 3
make 2 with 24
make 2 with 26

Fig. 4
make 2 with 32
make 2 with 34

Attach the two units with 17 half-square triangles to the top and bottom. Rotate the units so the teal half-square triangles are sewn against the strips. Press seam allowances toward the strips.

Sew the large rust triangles to the four sides of the center square unit (see the Quilt Assembly diagram). Sew them to opposite sides as you go.

NOTE: To avoid stretching, sew the pieces together with the triangle on the bottom, next to the sewing machine's feed dogs.

ROUND 3: Sew the two units with 24 half-square triangles units to opposite sides. Rotate the units so the rust half-square triangles are sewn against the square. Press seam allowances toward the square.

Sew the two units with 26 half-square triangles to the top and bottom of the square. Rotate the units so the rust half-square triangles are sewn against the square. Press seam allowances toward the square.

Middle Border

Pin and sew the 5" x 39½" teal rectangles to the sides of the center square.

Pin and sew the 5" x 48½" teal rectangles to the top and bottom.

ROUND 4: Sew the two units with 32 half-square triangles to opposite sides of the center square. Rotate the units so the teal half-square triangles are sewn against the strips. Press seam allowances toward the strips.

Sew the two units with 34 half-square triangles to the top and bottom of the center square. Rotate the units so the teal half-square triangles are sewn against the strips. Press seam allowances toward the strips.

Border

Measure the quilt top, including seam allowances. It should measure 51½" x 51½".

Trim the four 10" rust border pieces to your measurement. Pin and sew two border strips to the sides. Sew the 10¼" teal squares to both ends of the remaining two border strips. Attach to the top and bottom.

Quilting

The half-square triangles are machine quilted in the ditch. The large plain triangles and borders are quilted with wreaths and various cable designs.

Binding

This quilt has a finished ¾" binding. (See pg. 25 for binding techniques.)

Quilt Assembly

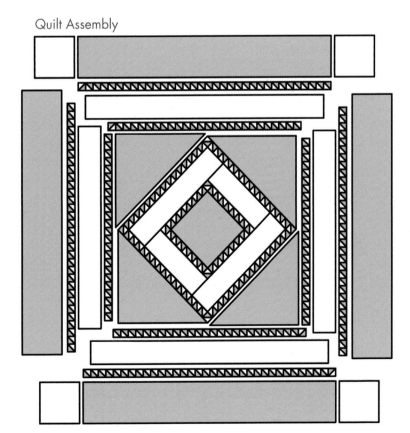

Barbara Dieges

WOVEN QUILT

One of our neighbors, Penny Sampson, is a weaver. It is something to watch her at the loom. That shuttle just flies cross the threads. It's like magic. I like what she does. Since I am not a weaver, I traded some of my quilts for her weaving. That's fair, I think, because she doesn't quilt.

When I look at her coverlets, the squares and rectangles look just like piecing! So I drafted up a block that looked like some of Penny's weaving and made this quilt.

When I took it to the next quilting bee, though, Jessie Turner told me it wasn't a new block. It looked just like another pattern she had seen before – Burgoyne Surrounded. She showed it to me in her book. It's supposed to be a block from the Revolutionary War.

I did have to agree, it had the same look with those squares and rectangles, but I used the squares in different places. Mine is a WOVEN QUILT.

Barbara Dieges

Finished size: 78" x 78"

Finished block size: 18"

Number of Blocks: Nine with sashing

Setting: Three by three blocks

Barbara Dieges

Amount/Fabric	Piece/Amount	1st Cut	Assembly
4¾ yds. – Muslin or Off-white print	Unit A Unit B and Cornerstones Sashing and Borders	(23) 1½" strips (16) 2½" strips (9) 4½" strips length of fabric (Cut 1, 4½" x 18½" rectangle off the end of four strips, set aside those four strips for borders, cut the remaining five strips into 20, 4½" x 18½" rectangles.)	Strip piecing (see instructions)

There are five print or plaid fabrics of different values in this quilt. They are listed according to their value and assigned a number, from very dark to a light medium.

Amount/Fabric	Piece/Amount	1st Cut	Assembly
1⅜ yds. – #1 red – very dark	Unit B Binding	(8) 1½" strips (10) 3½" strips length of fabric	Strip piecing (see instructions)
⅜ yd. – #2 red	Unit B Cornerstones	(1) 4½" strip (4) 1½" strips	
⅝ yd. – #3 red	Unit A and Unit B Unit A	(5) 2½" strips (5) 1½" strips	
⅜ yd. – #4 red	Unit A	(8) 1½" strips	
⅞ yd. – #5 red – lightest	Unit A Border squares	(10) 2½" strips (4) 4½" squares	
4⅞ yd.	Backing	(Seam the length of the quilt)	
82" x 82"	Batting		

The blocks for Woven Quilt are made from bands of fabric that have been sewn together, then cut into segments. For the units to match, it is very important that your cutting be accurate and that you sew with a scant ¼" seam allowance. As the strips are sewn together, press seam allowances toward the dark fabric.

UNIT A (Fig. 1): See strip piecing hints on pg. 8.

UNIT A, BAND A1 (Fig. 2): Assemble five bands of five strips each, sewn together in the following order, then cut into segments across the bands as indicated.
• 2½" #5 strip
• 1½" background strip
• 1½" #3 strip
• 1½" background strip
• 2½" #5 strip
Cut into 72, 2½" segments.

UNIT A, BAND A2 (Fig. 3): Sew three bands of five strips each together in the following order, then cut as indicated.
• 2½" background strip
• 1½" #4 strip
• 1½" background strip
• 1½" #4 strip
• 2½" background strip
Cut into 72, 1½" segments.

UNIT A, BAND A3 (Fig. 4): Sew two bands of five strips each following the order given below, then cut into segments as indicated.
• 2½" #3 strip
• 1½" background strip
• 1½" #4 strip
• 1½" background strip
• 2½" #3 strip
Cut into 36, 1½" segments.

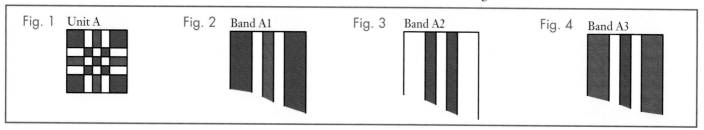

Fig. 1   Unit A   Fig. 2   Band A1   Fig. 3   Band A2   Fig. 4   Band A3

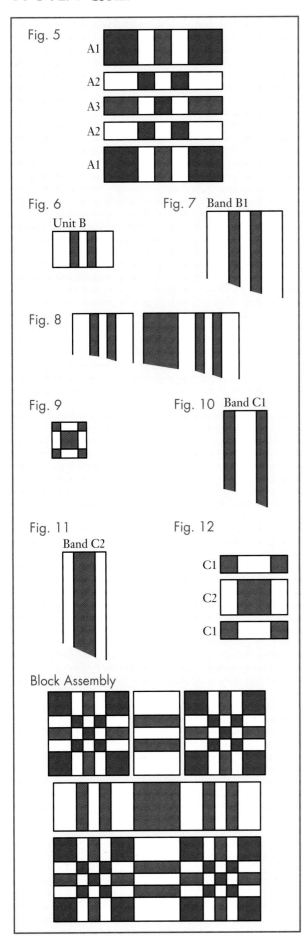

Fig. 5
A1
A2
A3
A2
A1

Fig. 6
Unit B

Fig. 7 Band B1

Fig. 8

Fig. 9

Fig. 10 Band C1

Fig. 11
Band C2

Fig. 12
C1
C2
C1

Block Assembly

(Fig. 5) Sew segments together as shown to make 36 of Unit A.

UNIT B (Fig. 6)

UNIT B, BAND B1 (Fig. 7): Sew four bands of five strips each in the following order, then cut into segments across the bands as indicated.
• 2½" background strip
• 1½" #1 strip
• 1½" background strip
• 1½" #1 strip
• 2½" background strip
Cut into 36, 4½" segments.

UNIT B, BAND B2 (Fig. 8): Sew one 4½" #2 strip between two, B1 Bands and cut into 9, 4½" segments.

CORNERSTONES (Fig. 9)

CORNERSTONES, BAND C1 (Fig. 10): Sew two bands together in the following order then cut segments across the bands as indicated.
• 1½" #2 strip
• 2½" background strip
• 1½" #2 strip
Cut into 32, 1½" segments.

CORNERSTONES, BAND C2 (Fig. 11): Sew one band together in the following order, then cut segments across the band as indicated.
• 1½" background strip
• 2½" #3 strip
• 1½" background strip
Cut into 16, 2½" segments.

(Fig. 12) Sew segments together to make 16 cornerstones.

Block Assembly
Sew a B1 unit between two A units, abutting seam allowances. Press seam allowances under Unit A. Make 18, A/B1 units, two for each block (see the Block Assembly diagram).

Sew a B2 unit between two A/B1 units to complete each block. Blocks should measure 18½" square.

Quilt Assembly
Sew three blocks between four sashing strips (see the Quilt Assembly diagram). Press seam allowances toward the blocks. Make three rows.

Sew three sashing strips between four cornerstone units. Press the seam allowances toward the cornerstones. Make four rows. Sew the rows together, alternating sashing rows and block rows.

Border
Measure the height and width of the quilt top. It should measure 70½" square. Cut the four, 4½" border strips to your measurement. Pin and sew two strips to the sides.

Sew a 4½" #5 square to both ends of the remaining two border strips. Pin and sew to the top and bottom, abutting the seams of the side borders.

Quilting
This quilt has cross hatching in the pieced blocks and feathers in the sashing and borders.

Binding
The quilt has a finished ½" binding. See pg. 25 for binding techniques.

Quilt Assembly

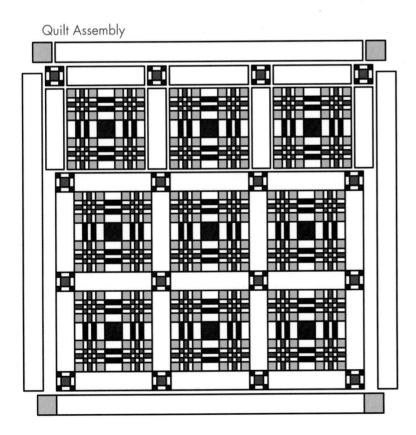

Quilting pattern

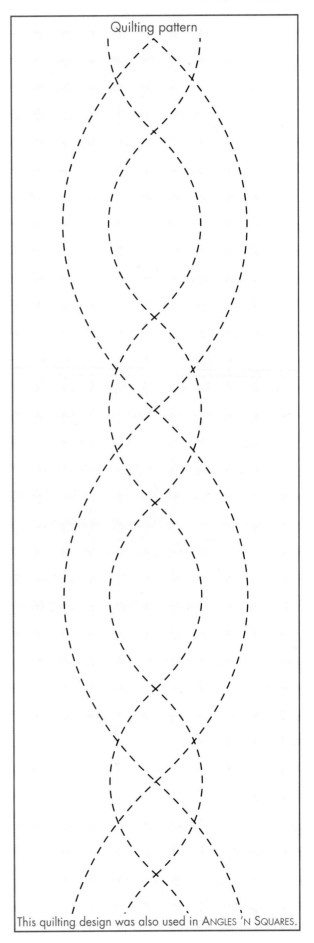

This quilting design was also used in ANGLES 'N SQUARES.

CHERRY picking SUMMERS

When I look at this quilt, I think of all those cherry picking summers. The children would climb up in the old cherry tree. More cherries ended up in their mouths than in the baskets.

They would fight off the bluebirds and robins. The birds thought they had first claim to those cherries and did not want to share.

We always took a basket of cherries down to Mrs. Pearson on the next parcel. She was all alone there except for a farmhand or two. Whenever we visited, she had the same oatmeal sweets for the little ones. She said there was something special in them.

When she finally gave me the recipe, that something special was chopped up raisins. She chopped them so fine, you never knew they were in there. It did make them taste very special. I still make them. When I have one of those sweets, it brings back all the memories.

When it came to quilting this quilt, I used some patterns that Papa had painted on the children's cradle, there, in between the cherries.

Just like I couldn't make the same quilt twice, I couldn't do the same quilting pattern either. I always had to make something different.

Barbara Dieges

Finished size: 68" x 68"
Finished block size: 9"

Number of blocks: 25 blocks in
five different designs
Setting: Medallion style

Barbara Dieges

Amount/Fabric	Piece/Amount	1st Cut	2nd Cut	Assembly
3⅜ yds. – Tea dyed muslin or very light beige print	(Cut the yardage into two pieces – one 2-yard piece and one 1⅜ yard piece)			
2 yd. length	**Borders**	(4) 7" strips length of fabric		
	Blocks A, C & E			
	Appliqué squares and rectangles	(2) 7" strips length of fabric (4) 7" x 13" rectangles	(12) 7" squares and	
1⅜ yd. length	**Blocks A, B, D & E**			
	Half–square Triangles	(3) 7¾" strips	(14) 7¾" squares	(HSTM – pg. 18)
	Block B, D			
	Corner triangles	(2) 6⅞" strips	(8) 6⅞" squares	(Cut once diagonally)
	Block C, D, E	(3) 3⅞" strips	(28) 3⅞" squares	(FG – pg. 18)
		(1) 7¼" square		(FG – pg. 18)
¼ yd. – #1 Blue	**Block A & C**	(1) 7¼" square		(SqP – pg. 19)
		(1) 7¾" square		(HSTM – pg. 18)
¼ yd. – #2 Blue	**Block C**	(2) 7¼" squares		(FG – pg. 18)
½ yd. – #3 Blue	**Block D**			
	Small triangles	(1) 3⅞" strip	(8) 3⅞" squares	(Cut once diagonally)
	Large triangle	(1) 13¼" square	(Cut twice diagonally)	
	Half–square triangles	(2) 7¾" squares		(HSTM – pg. 18)
1 yd. – #4 Blue	**Block A, B, E**			
	Half–square triangles	(2) 7¾" strips	(10) 7¾" squares	(HSTM – pg. 18)
	Block B			
	Lg. corner triangle – 8	(1) 6⅞" strip	(4) 6⅞" squares	(Cut once diagonally)
	Small triangles – 16	(1) 3⅞" strip	(8) 3⅞" squares	(Cut once diagonally)
¼ yd. each – Three red prints	**Appliqué – Cherries**	88 of Cherry template – pg. 83	Cut 30 from each fabric	
¼ yd. each – Three browns	**Appliqué – Stems**	(8) ¾" bias strips		
¼ yd. each – Two green prints	**Appliqué – Leaves**	72 of Leaf template 5 – pg. 83		
½ yd. each – Green print	**Border vines**	(8) 1" bias strips		
1¼ yd.	**Binding**	(6) 3½" strips length of fabric		
4¼ yd.	**Backing**	Seam the length or width of the quilt		
72" x 72"	**Batting**			

This quilt has five different blocks, some that use the same units as other blocks.

Appliqué

Although three red fabrics for the cherries and two greens for the leaves are called for, this is a good opportunity to use a variety of reds and greens.

Complete all the appliqué before piecing the blocks. Before piecing the blocks, appliqué the cherry clusters onto the background squares, rectangles, and borders, following the circle appliqué instructions on pg. 14. Follow the block designs on pg. 83 and transfer the cherry cluster designs to the 7" x 13" rectangles and 7" squares.

Pay careful attention to the design orientation in the block designs – the cherry clusters are not positioned in a mirror image arrangement.

APPLIQUÉ – STEMS: Prepare ¾" bias strips for the stems. The stems are sewn first to the background squares and rectangles.

APPLIQUÉ – VINES: Make four vines of bias strips by sewing two of the cut bias strips together end to end. Follow Vine/Stem #1 instructions (pg. 13). Baste the vines to the border strips, then appliqué the stems. The basted vine helps with the placement of the stems. The stem ends can be tucked underneath and the vine appliquéd in place. The leaves are placed over the vine.

APPLIQUÉ – LEAVES: Cut a total of 72 leaves, 36 leaves

from each green fabric. The leaves and cherries are appliquéd last.

APPLIQUÉ – CHERRIES: Cut templates from heavy paper such as 4" x 5" cards.

Make 88 cherry appliqué pieces by cutting 29 or 30, 2" circles from each red fabric. Make a concave cut on each circle so it looks like the fabric template. Then follow Appliqué Circle instructions on pg. 14.

Trim appliqué squares to 6½" and trim appliqué rectangles to 6½" x 12½" after appliquéing.

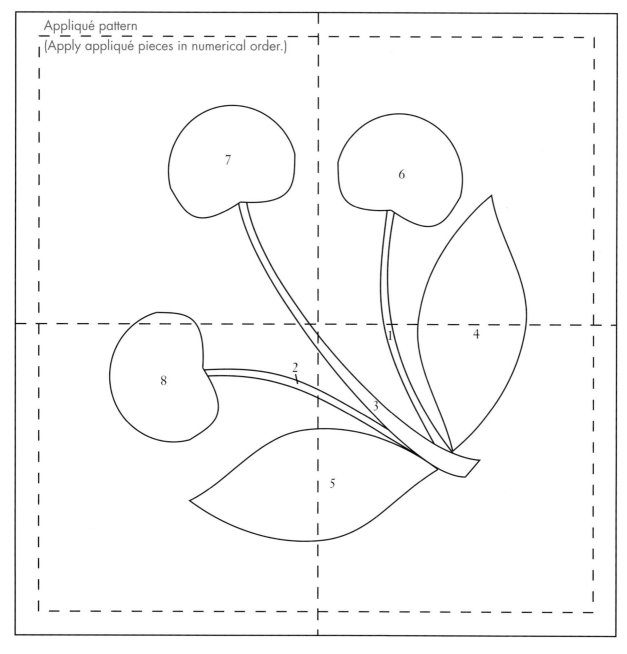

Appliqué pattern
(Apply appliqué pieces in numerical order.)

Unit Assembly

MULTIPLE HALF-SQUARE TRIANGLES: Layer the 7¾" background squares with the 7¾" squares of #1, #2, and #4 blue.

Make multiple half-square triangles following the instructions on pg. 18. Keep like fabric triangles together.

FLYING GEESE:
Following the Flying Geese method on pg. 18, assemble Flying Geese units using the following combinations:
- one, 7¼" background square and four, 3⅞" #4 blue squares;
- one, 7¼" #3 blue square and four, 3⅞" background squares;
- two, 7¼" #2 blue squares and eight, 3⅞" background squares.

SQUARE ON POINT: For the center block, make a square on-point following the directions on pg. 19. Use one, 7¼" #1 blue square and four, 3⅞" background squares. Be sure to sew a second seam ½" toward the corner from the first diagonal seam when attaching the smaller squares, then cut between the two stitching lines. The four bonus half-square triangle units generated by making the square on-point unit will be used for the corner cherry blocks.

Block A Assembly (Fig. 1)

There are eight Block A units in two colorways. Make four Block A Medium units from:
- five, #4 blue pieced half-square triangles;
- one, cherry appliqué block.

Arrange the five pieced half-square triangles around a cherry appliqué block. Place the appliqué block in the same position for each block.

Make four Block A Dark units in the same manner, using:
- five, #1 blue half-square triangles;
- one, cherry appliqué block.

Block B Assembly (Fig. 2)

Each Block B (North Wind) requires:
- two small triangles cut from a 3⅞" background square;
- two small triangles cut from a 3⅞" #4 blue square;
- one large triangle cut from a 6⅞" background square;
- one large triangle cut from a 6⅞" #4 blue square; and
- three #4 blue pieced half-square triangles.

Sew the small cut triangles to the sides of #4 blue pieced half-square triangles as shown. Press seam allowances under the darker fabric.

Sew the half-square triangle units together. Attach the large background and #4 blue triangles last. Make eight blocks.

Block C Assembly (Fig. 3)

Block C requires:
- four, cherry appliqué blocks;
- eight, #2 blue Flying Geese units;
- one, square-on-point unit.

Arrange the cherry appliqué blocks and Flying Geese units around the square-on-point unit as shown, being careful to give each appliqué block a quarter turn around the center. Sew units together to make one block.

Block D (Fig. 4)

There are four Block D units. Each requires:
- four small triangles cut from two, 3⅞" background squares;
- four small triangles cut from two, 3⅞" #3 blue squares;
- one large triangle cut from a 13¼" #3 blue square;
- two corner triangles cut from a 6⅞" background square;
- one Flying Geese unit made from the 7¼" #3 background square;
- four blue 3⅞" squares;
- four #3 blue pieced half-square triangles.

Make four blocks.

Block E (Fig. 5)

Each Block E requires:
- one cherry appliqué rectangle;
- eight #4 blue pieced half-square triangles;
- one #4 blue Flying Geese unit made from the 7¼" background square;
- four, 3⅞" #4 blue squares.

Assemble as shown and press all seam allowances toward the dark fabric. Make four blocks.

Quilt Top Assembly

Assemble rows of five blocks each as shown in the Quilt Assembly diagram.

Borders

Measure the quilt top. It should measure 54½" square. Attach appliquéd border strips to the quilt top following the mitered border directions on pg. 20.

Quilting

This quilt features diagonal crosshatching at 1" and 2" intervals in the background along with a few country motifs. It is also quilted in the ditch around the patches and appliqué.

Binding

The quilt has a ½" binding. See pg. 25 for information about bindings.

Cherry Appliqué pattern

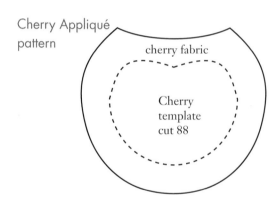

Leaf Appliqué pattern

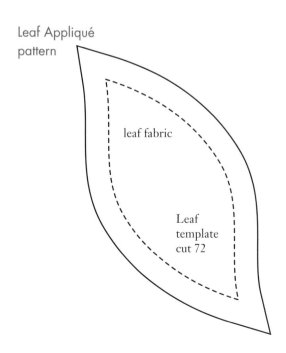

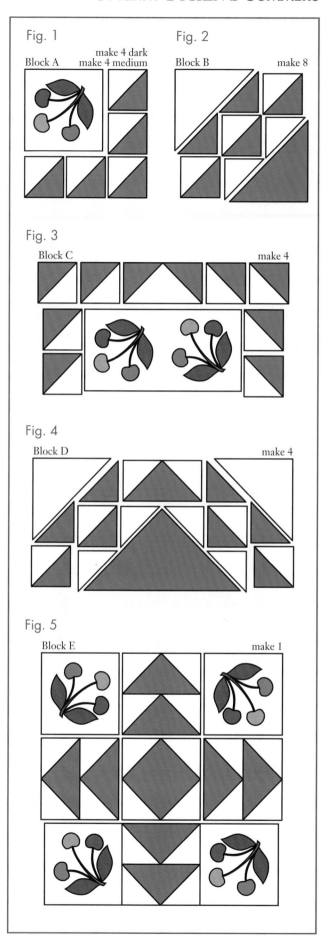

CHERRY PICKING SUMMERS

Border Assembly diagram

center

Detail of CHERRY PICKING SUMMERS

Quilt Assembly diagram

Barbara Dieges

It was early in the evening, going on to suppertime. The animals were put up and we were all in the house.

"Ma, Pa, a bear!" Ethan yelped, getting our attention.

"A what?"

"A bear, out at the water trough."

Sure enough there was a bear, a young one, slaking his thirst. There wasn't a sound from the barn. He raised his head, sniffed round and drank some more.

"Aren't you going to shoot him, Pa?"

"We'll watch him," John answered. "Go to the bedroom and see which way he's headed. He's probably going down to the berry patches. It isn't right to kill an animal when he's at the water. He hasn't done us any harm. If he heads up to the barn, that's different."

John was that way. We were out in the wilderness and had to be careful of bear and panther. He'd hunt for food, but wouldn't kill needlessly.

It was strange about the bears. Until then we hadn't seen any and didn't after that for a long time. Neighbors up the road a piece had a lot of trouble with bears – went after their animals. They'd shoot them, but the bears didn't seem to bother us. So I thought this Bear's Paw quilt would be a good one to make.

Barbara Dieges

Finished size: 73" x 84"

Finished block size: 10½"

Number of blocks: 30 with sashing

Setting: Five by six blocks

A Thread *runs* **through it**

Barbara Dieges

Fabric and cutting instructions are given for two variations of this Bear's Paw quilt. The background fabric is the same for both variations. The first variation uses 20 different fat quarters for a scrappy look. The inner border for this variation is pieced.

The coordinated block variation uses two fabrics, a medium and a dark. The inner border of this version uses sashing strips and cornerstones.

Amount/Fabric	Piece/Amount	1st Cut	2nd Cut	Assembly
2½ yds. – Very light print or muslin	**Blocks – background**			
	Half-square triangles	(8) 4¾" strips	(60) 4¾" squares	(HSTM – pg. 18)
	Rectangles	(15) 2" strips	(120) 2" x 5" rectangles	
	Small squares	(7) 2" strips	(140) 2" squares	
	Small squares and Cornerstones	(7) 2" strips for coordinated blocks variation only. Cut 162, 2" squares		
	(Coordinated quilt requires two additional 2" strips for 22 more squares.)			
Scrappy Quilt 10 fat quarters – Medium prints/plaids	**Blocks**			
	half-square triangles	(6) 4¾" squares per fabric		(HSTM – pg. 18)
		(1) 2" x 5" rectangle per fabric		
		(1) 2" x 8" rectangle per fabric		
10 fat quarters – Dark prints/plaids	Squares – 120	(12) 3½" squares per fabric		(HSTM – pg. 18)
	Sashing – rectangles	(2) 2" x 11" rectangles per fabric		
	Inner Border	(2) 2" squares per fabric		
		(1) 2" x 5" rectangle per fabric		
		(1) 2" x 8" rectangle per fabric		
1 fat quarter – Dark print	**Blocks**			
	Center squares	(3) 2" strips	(30) 2" squares	
Coordinated Blocks Variation 2 yds. – Med. print/plaid	**Blocks**			
2 yds. – Dk. print/plaid				
	Half-square triangles	(4) 4¾" strips per fabric	(60) 4¾" squares per fabric	(HSTM – pg. 18)
	Lg. squares	(6) 3½" strips per fabric	(120) 3½" squares	
	Sashing – rectangles	(14) 2" strips per fabric	(49) 2" x 11" rectangles	
1 fat quarter – Dark print	**Blocks**			
	Center squares	(3) 2" strips	(30) 2" squares	
2½ yds. – Dk. print/plaid	**Outer border**	(4) 6" strips length of fabric		
1 yd.	**Binding**	(10) 3½" strips length of fabric		
5⅛ yds.	**Backing**	Seam the length of the quilt		
77" x 88"	**Batting**			

Unit Assembly

HALF-SQUARE TRIANGLES: Layer the 4¾" background squares with the 4¾" plaid squares, right sides together. Make pieced half-square triangles following the multiples method on pg. 18. Each block requires 16 half-square triangles.

(Fig. 1) Chain sew 120, 2" background squares together with half-square triangles as shown.

(Fig. 2) Sew a matching half-square triangle to the first unit paying attention to the alignment. Press seam allowances under the dark triangles.

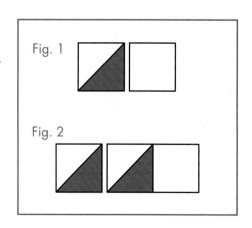

Fig. 1

Fig. 2

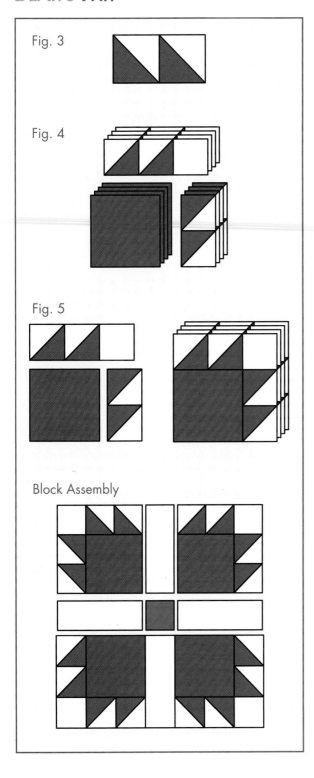

Fig. 3

Fig. 4

Fig. 5

Block Assembly

(Fig. 3) Chain sew 240 half-square triangles into pairs, being careful to pair like colors together.

(Fig. 4) For each block, match and stack four long and short units of the same fabrics. Stack four matching 3½" plaid squares together.

(Fig. 5) Sew the short unit to the side of each 3½" plaid square. Press the seam allowances so they lay under the darker fabric. Sew the long unit to the side. Make four units for each block.

Block Assembly

Sew a 2" x 5" background rectangle between two pairs of "paws," making certain the paws are facing away from each other (Block Assembly diagram). Press seam allowances under the paws. Make two of these units for each block.

Sew a 2" center square between two, 2" x 5" rectangles for each block.

Sew a sashing unit between two paws units, rotating one unit so it faces away from the other one. Repeat for all of the blocks. Press seam allowances under the paws.

Sashing

(Fig. 6) Sew four, 2" background cornerstones between five, 2" x 11" plaid rectangles. Make five sashing strips to be sewn between the six vertical rows of blocks.

Arrange the blocks in six rows of five blocks each.

Sew four, 2" x 11" rectangles between five blocks in each row. Make six rows (see the Quilt Assembly diagram).

Sew the six vertical rows together, alternating with plaid sashing strips. Match seams.

Inner Border – Scrappy Quilt Variation

Sew the 2" squares, 2" x 5" and 2" x 8" rectangles of the various fabrics into a strip a minimum of 275" in length. Mix up the pieces randomly as you go. There should be some extra length. If not, cut more 2" strips.

Fig. 6

Measure the height of the quilt top. It should measure 71". From your pieced strip cut two pieces the height of the quilt top. Adjust the strip so the cut is not too close to a seam. Pin and sew to the sides.

Measure the width of the quilt top including borders and seam allowance. It should measure 62". Cut two strips to your measurement. Pin and sew to the top and bottom.

Inner Border – Coordinated Blocks Variation

Sew 2" x 11" rectangles of medium and dark plaids together alternately with 2" background squares. Make two border strips of six, 2" x 11" rectangles and five, 2" background squares. Attach them to the sides of the quilt top. Match seams with the setting strip seams.

Sew two border strips of six, 2" squares and five, 2" x 11" rectangles (see Coordinated Quilt diagram). Attach to the top and bottom of the quilt top. Match seams.

Outer Border

Measure the height of the quilt top. It should measure 74". Cut two, 6" strips to your measurement. Pin and sew to the sides.

Measure the width of the quilt top including borders and seam allowances. It should measure 73". Cut the remaining two, 6" strips to your measurement. Pin and sew to the top and bottom.

Quilting

The pieced blocks are quilted in the ditch and cable designs were quilted in the sashings and border.

Binding

The quilt has a finished ½" binding. See pg. 25 for binding techniques. This quilt would also look good with a plaid binding, cut on the bias to take advantage of the resulting diagonal design. Attach bias binding carefully to avoid stretching the strip.

Quilt Assembly

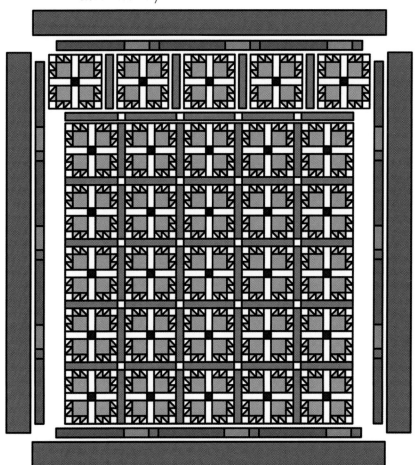

PATRIOTIC PUZZLE

We've had some hard times here in Thistle Hollow. There were some long, hard winters when we thought there would be no end to the snow. There was that spring of '98 when our stores of food ran so low that we were eating griddle cakes at every meal and split pea soup without the ham.

We just all helped each other and shared what we had – even hay for the animals – when someone ran low.

Then there were the good times. One of those was Independence Day. Now, that was celebrating! We'd come together for fireworks, music, dancing, singing, and eating. Everyone brought a big basket of food.

Here is how this PATRIOTIC PUZZLE quilt came about. Usually, when it came to making a quilt, I'd be using pieces from my piecing bag. Seldom had a big enough piece for a whole quilt, unless it was muslin.

At the general store, I saw this bolt of red goods. It was a fine piece of calico. Thought maybe I'd get just a little piece – not much. Then I thought better of it. John must have noticed, but he didn't say anything.

I must say I was very surprised to see that whole bolt come out of the wagon and into the house when we got home.

I asked him, "How can we afford all that? There are other things we need."

"Never you mind," he said. "Sometimes there are more important things than need. I saw how you were when you were looking at it. Anyway, I worked it out with Mr. Jenson. And besides, I like red."

He had traded some cabinet work for that bolt.

The blue came from a dress of Rebecca's and now I had plenty of red! It found its way into a lot of quilts, dresses, shirts, aprons, and even curtains.

Barbara Dieges

Finished size: 56" x 72"
Finished block size: 6"

Number of blocks: 35 alternating blocks
Setting: Five by seven with pieced sashing

Barbara Dieges

Amount/Fabric	Piece/Amount	1st Cut	2nd Cut	Assembly
1½ yds. – Very light or white print	Blocks & Four-Patch units	(16) 2" strips (5) 3½" strips	Strip piecing Strip piecing	(See instructions) (See instructions)
4¼ yds. – Dk. or red print	Blocks Flying Geese Border (cut from 2 yd. length)	(10) 2" strips (5) 3½" strips (9) 3⅞" strips (4) 3½" strips length of fabric	Strip piecing Strip piecing (82) 3⅞" squares	(See instructions) (See instructions) (FG – pg. 18)
1⅝ yds. – Med. or blue	Four-Patch units Flying Geese	(5) 2" strips (6) 7¼" strips	(21) 7¼" squares	(FP – pg. 18) (FG – pg. 18)
1 yd. – Dk. or red print	Binding	(9) 2¾" strips length of fabric		
3⅝ yds.	Backing	Seam across the quilt width		
60" x 76"	Batting			

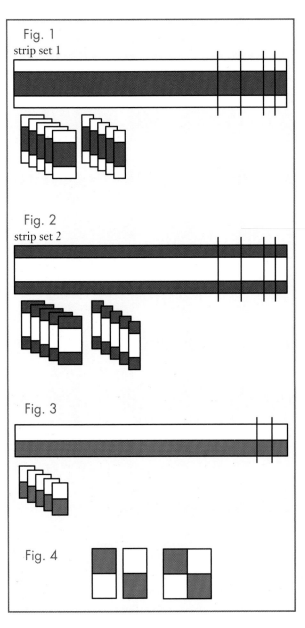

Fig. 1
strip set 1

Fig. 2
strip set 2

Fig. 3

Fig. 4

Strip Piecing
(Fig. 1) Sew a 2" light fabric strip on both sides of a 3½" dark fabric strip. Make five of these strip sets. Press seam allowances under the dark fabric. From the strip sets cut:
• 17, 3½" segments;
• 36, 2" segments.

(Fig. 2) Sew a 2" dark fabric strip on both sides of a 3½" light fabric strip. Make five strip sets. Press seam allowances under the dark fabric. From the strip sets cut:
• 18, 3½" segments;
• 34, 2" segments.

(Fig. 3) Sew a 2" light strip and a 2" medium strip together. Make five strip sets. Press seam allowances under the medium fabric.
From the strip sets cut:
• 104, 2" segments.

Four-Patch Units
(Fig. 4) Sew the 2" light/medium segments together to make 52 Four-Patch units.

Flying Geese Units
Following the instructions on pg. 18, use the 3⅞" dark squares and the 7¼" medium squares to make 82 Flying Geese units.

Quilt Assembly

(Fig. 5) Sew a 2" strip set 1 segment to either side of a 3½" strip set 2 segment, abutting the seam allowances.

(Fig. 6) Sew a 2" strip set 2 segment to either side of a 3½" strip set 1 segment, abutting the seam allowances.

Sew the patches into 15 rows alternating with the Flying Geese (see the Quilt Assembly diagram), being careful to orient the patches exactly as shown.

Connect the rows together, repeating a sequence of rows 1–4 (see the Quilt Assembly diagram).

Border

Measure the height and width of the quilt top, including seam allowances. It should measure 48½" x 66½". Cut two 3½" strips to your height measurement and sew to the sides.

Cut the remaining two 3½" strips to your width measurement. Sew the remaining Four-Patch units to the ends of these strips. Align them so the light patches will connect with the light corner patches in the quilt top. Sew the strips to the top and bottom of the quilt top.

Quilting

PATRIOTIC PUZZLE is quilted with diagonal lines and a continuous loop design.

Binding

This quilt has a finished ⅜" binding. See pg. 25 for binding techniques.

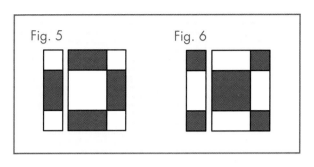

Fig. 5   Fig. 6

Quilt Assembly

My wild ROSE

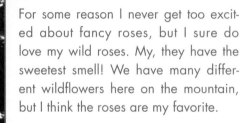

For some reason I never get too excited about fancy roses, but I sure do love my wild roses. My, they have the sweetest smell! We have many different wildflowers here on the mountain, but I think the roses are my favorite.

John dug up some from down by the stream and put them where I can see them every day. This pink made me think of those pretty little roses; wild roses only have five petals. The new leaves are this shade of green in the spring. Then in the fall, I gather the hips to make a good tasting tea.

I mixed the rose petals with some of my lavender. Sprinkled the mix in between my linens to make them smell pretty.

So this is MY WILD ROSE.

Barbara Dieges

Finished size: 82¼" x 102¾"
Finished block size: 11¼"
Number of blocks: 18

Setting: Three by four blocks set
diagonally with 3" sashing

Barbara Dieges

Amount/Fabric	Piece/Amount	1st Cut	2nd Cut	Assembly
5½ yds. – White	**Background**			
	Appliqué Blocks	(4) 7¼" strips	(18) 7¼" squares	
	Blocks			
	Half-square triangles	(6) 4" strips	(54) 4" squares	(HSTM – pg. 18)
	Flying Geese	(2) 3½" strips	(18) 3½" squares	(FG – pg. 18)
	Corner squares	(3) 1⅝" strips	(72) 1⅝" squares	
	Sashing and	(23) 1½" strips	Strip piecing	(see instructions)
	Nine-Patch units	(8) 3½" strips	(24) 3½" x 11¾" rectangles	
	Edge Triangles	(2) 21½" strips	(3) 21½" squares	Cut twice diagonally
	Corner Triangles	(1) 13⅛" strip	(2) 13⅛" squares	Cut once diagonally
⅜ yd. each – Nine green prints	**Blocks –**			
	Triangles	(2) 5⅜" squares per fabric	Once diagonally	
	Half-square triangles	(6) 4" squares per fabric		(HSTM – pg. 18)
	Flying Geese	(4) 2" squares per fabric		(FG – pg. 18)
	Template A	2 from each fabric		
	Sashing	(2) 1½" strips per fabric		
¼ yd. – Nine pink prints	**Blocks – Template B**	10 from each fabric		
	Sashing and	(2) 1½" strips from two fabrics		
	Nine-Patch units			
Scraps – Dark gold	**Blocks – Template C**	Cut 18		
Scraps – Dark brown print	**Blocks – Template D**	Cut 18		
⅜ yd. – Pink	**Inner Border**	(8) 1½" strips		
2½ yds. – Green print	**Outer Border**	(4) 8" strips length of fabric		
	Cornerstones	(4) 1½" squares		
1 yd. – Green print	**Binding**	(12) 3½" strips length of fabric		
6¼ yds.	**Backing**	Seam the length of the quilt		
86" x 107"	**Batting**			

Appliqué

Appliqué the 18 background blocks following the general instructions beginning on pg. 9. Layer the appliqué pieces in alphabetical order following the schematic on pg. 99. After appliquéing the squares, trim them to a uniform 6⅞" square.

Half-square Triangles

Use 4" background squares and 4" green squares to make 432 of these units. Follow the multiple half-square triangle method on pg. 18.

Make 72 units of three half-square triangles (see the Block Assembly diagram). Orient the green triangles to the left.

Make 72 units of three half-square triangles with the green triangles pointing to the right.

NOTE: After sewing and cutting, each half-square triangle should measure 1⅝" square, including seam allowances.

Flying Geese

Use 2" green squares and 3½" background squares to make 72 pieced Flying Geese (see pg. 18 for instructions).

Sew each Flying Geese unit between two half-square triangle units (see the Block Assembly diagram). Make four units for each block.

Sew 1⅝" background squares to both ends of 36 triangle-Geese units.

Block Assembly

Match the fabrics of the outer units and triangles for each block.

(Fig. 1) Fold two large triangles in half and pinch or crease each one on the long edge. Pinch the square at the center of each side. Match the creases, pin, and sew.

Sew two large triangles to the opposing sides of the square, matching the creases.

Machine sew with the square on top and the triangle on the bottom to minimize stretching. The triangle corners will protrude beyond the square about the same amount on each side.

Sew the half-square triangle/Flying Geese units to the top and bottom of the center. Sew the triangle/Geese/square units to the sides (see the Block Assembly diagram).

Sashing and cornerstones

The outer sashing and cornerstones of the quilt utilize the same pink and green fabrics as the blocks, so the 11¾" segments and Nine-Patch cornerstones are all different.

SEWING SASHING (Fig. 2): Sew one, 1½" green strip between two, 1½" background strips. Repeat, making eight strip units. From these units, cut 24, 11¾" segments for the outer sashing.

(Fig. 3) Sew one, 1½" background strip between two, 1½" green strips. Repeat, making three strip units. Cut 62, 1½" segments.

(Fig. 4) Sew one, 1½" pink strip between two, 1½" background strips. Make two strip units. Cut 31, 1½" segments.

(Fig. 5) Sew one pink/background segment between two green/background segments. Make 31 Nine-Patch units.

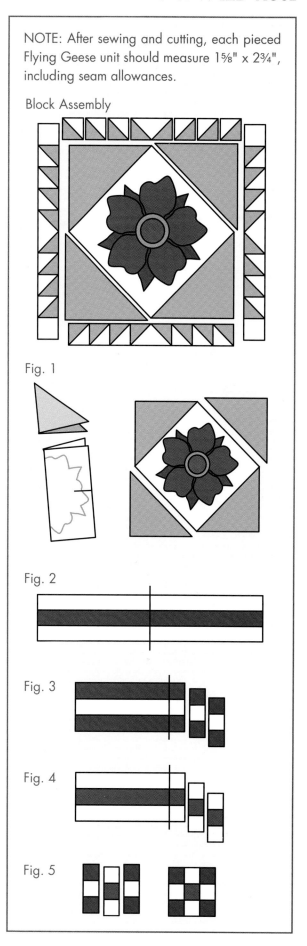

NOTE: After sewing and cutting, each pieced Flying Geese unit should measure 1⅝" x 2¾", including seam allowances.

Block Assembly

Fig. 1

Fig. 2

Fig. 3

Fig. 4

Fig. 5

Quilt Assembly

When sewing blocks together in a diagonal set, treat the blocks as if they were being sewn into horizontal rows with the exception that each row has a different number of blocks (see the Quilt Assembly diagram). This quilt has two corner units and four rows of blocks. The edge triangles are sewn on the ends of the rows. Half of the rows are rotated and then sewn together. Sew together the sashing units as shown on the Quilt Assembly diagram.

Borders

INNER BORDER: Join two inner border strips together with a diagonal joining to make four, 1½" border strips. Measure the height and width of the quilt top including seam allowances. It should measure 65¼" x 85⅜". Trim two strips to your height measurement. Pin and sew to the sides.

Trim two inner border strips to your width measurement and sew a 1½" square to both ends of the strips. Pin and sew to the top and bottom, matching seams. The seam allowances should abut.

OUTER BORDER: Measure the height of the quilt top including borders and seam allowances. It should measure 87⅜". Trim two, 8" outer border strips to your measurement. Pin and sew to the sides.

Measure the width including borders and seam allowances. It should measure 82¼". Trim two outer border strips to your measurement. Pin and sew to the top and bottom.

Quilting

This quilt is quilted diagonally in the ditch. Feathers are quilted in the plain sashing and other designs in the edge triangles. Since the border print is so large and busy, detailed quilting would not show so straight diagonal quilting lines are used instead. If the fabric choice had been a small print or a solid, a large cable design would have been appropriate.

Binding

This quilt has a finished ½" binding. See pg. 25 for binding techniques.

Quilt Assembly

Barbara Dieges

Cut a 2⅜" circle for C.
Cut a 1¾" circle for D.

B

B

A

B

C

D

B

B

B

Cut 18, 7¼" background squares.
After appliquéing, trim to 6⅞".

WEDDING RING

When we had been married 30 years, I made a quilt to celebrate. This WEDDING RING block was in Jessie's book. I made a block for each year. It is also called the Crown of Thorns. I guess it all depends on the marriage.

I hadn't entered anything into the county fair that year, but John suggested going to the fair after church. He knew that I would want to see the quilts.

We saw all the sights. There were all kinds of contests, from log-pulling to pie eating. Some women brought cakes and pies for judging. Farmers brought their animals to be judged and sold at auction. The cows, pigs, chickens, and sheep were making all kinds of commotion.

We finally came to the quilts. There were a lot of them and I was taking it all in. Then we came around a corner and there right in front of me was my quilt, with a big blue ribbon. I couldn't say a word; I was so surprised.

John said with a big grin, "Since you hadn't entered anything, I thought I'd do it for you!" He was very proud of my quilting. So he had slipped this quilt out without my knowing about it.

Barbara Dieges

Finished size: 85" x 98¼"
Finished block size: 9⅜"

Number of blocks: 30 with 20 alternate blocks
Setting: Five by six blocks on point

Barbara Dieges

WEDDING RING

The background of this quilt is the same throughout. Ten medium to dark fabrics are used for the 30 patchwork blocks.

Amount/Fabric	Piece/Amount	1st Cut	2nd Cut	Assembly
3¾ yds. – Very lt. print or muslin	**Alternate Blocks**	(5) 9⅞" strips	(20) 9⅞" squares	
	Blocks			
	Half–square triangles	(9) 5½" strips	(60) 5½" squares	(HSTM – pg. 18)
	Center squares	(2) 2⅜" strips	(30) 2⅜" squares	
	Square units	(10) 2⅜" strips	Strip piecing	(see instructions)
1¾ yds. – Print slightly darker than background	**Edge Blocks**	(6) 9⅞ strips	(22) 9⅞" squares	
10 fat quarters – Med. to dark prints/plaids	**Blocks**			
	Half–square triangles	(6) 5½" squares per fabric		(HSTM – pg. 18)
	Square units	(1) 2⅜" strip per fabric	Strip piecing	(see instructions)
2¾ yds. – Med. print	**Outer Borders**	(4) 3" strips length of fabric		
	Setting Triangles	(3) 14½" strips	(6) 14½" squares – Cut twice diagonally	
		(2) 7½" squares	Cut once diagonally	
1 yd. – Med. print	**Binding**	(12) 3½" strips length of fabric		
6 yds.	**Backing**	Seam the length of the quilt		
89" x 108"	**Batting**			

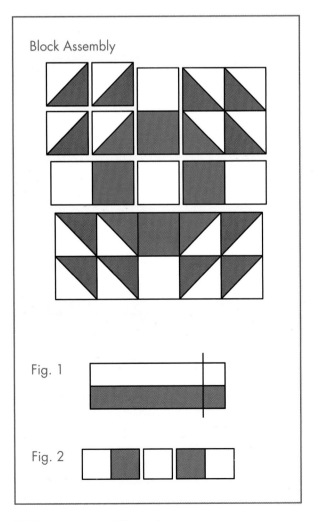

Block Assembly

Fig. 1

Fig. 2

Unit Assembly

HALF-SQUARE TRIANGLES: Layer each 5½" background square with a 5½" square of medium/dark fabric. Follow the multiple half-square triangle method on pg. 18 to make 480 pieced half-square triangles.

CORNER UNITS: Lay out three matching pieced half-square triangles and a fourth with a different fabric to form a Four-Patch unit (see the Block Assembly diagram).

Make 12 identical units. Four identical units are required for each block, so three blocks have the same fabrics. In each unit, each of the different half-square triangles should be aligned in the same corner.

SQUARE/STRIP SEGMENT (Fig. 1): Sew a 2⅜" medium or dark strip to each of 10, 2⅜" background strips.

Cut 12, 2⅜" segments from each of the 10 strip sets to make square/strip segments. Four matching segments are needed for each block. Leftover strips can be used for another project.

(Fig. 2) Sew a 2⅜" background square between two matching square/strip segments. Press seam allowances towards the darker fabric.

Barbara Dieges

Lay out the units as shown in the Block Assembly diagram. Match fabrics in strip and triangle units. Make sure the darker half of each square/strip segment is at the center of the block. Press seam allowances under the strip segments. Make 30 blocks.

Quilt Assembly

Assemble the blocks in diagonal rows (see the Quilt Assembly diagram). Also refer to page 20 for diagonal settings. Sew the rows together, being careful to match seams. Add setting triangles as shown. Add the corner triangles last.

Borders

Measure the height of the quilt top, including seam allowances. It should measure 93¼". Trim two, 3" border strips to your measurement. Pin and sew to the sides.

Measure the width, including borders and seam allowances. It should measure 85". Trim the remaining two border strips to your measurement. Pin and sew to the top and bottom.

Quilting

Two sizes of circles are quilted in the patch blocks. The square and octagon design in the center of the pieced blocks is quilted in the ditch. The plain squares allow for some intricate quilting. This quilt has a circular design with four bells. Diagonal lines at 1" intervals are quilted in the outer triangles and border. Feathered wreaths in the plain squares and an undulating design for a border would also be attractive.

Binding

The quilt has a finished ½" binding. See pg. 25 for information on binding techniques.

Quilt Assembly

SQUARE DANCING

This quilt reminds me of all the dancing I didn't do.

John and I danced at our wedding, but somehow, we just didn't do much afterwards. Even when we went to gatherings and there was dancing music, we didn't dance.

I don't think he felt comfortable out there sashaying around. He'd tap his foot to the music or play the dulcimer and sing the old songs, but he wouldn't dance. I don't know why. I never asked him about it.

So this is my SQUARE DANCING quilt. Those blocks make me think of a pair of dancers, the men in dark clothes and the women in light, twirling around to the music.

Barbara Dieges

Finished size: 53½" x 71½"
Finished block size: 9"

Number of blocks: 17 Jacob's Ladder
blocks and 18 Virginia Reel blocks
Setting: Five by seven

Barbara Dieges

Amount/Fabric	Piece/Amount	Cut	Assembly
9 fat quarters – Very light prints	**Jacob's Ladder Blocks** Half-square triangles Four-Patch units **Virginia Reel Blocks** Rectangles Four-Patch on point	(1) 7¾" square per fabric (2) 2" strips per fabric (2) 3⅛" x 7⅝" rectangles per fabric (1) 6½" square per fabric (2) 5⅝" squares per fabric (2) 3⅛" squares per fabric	(HSTM – pg. 18) (HSTM – pg. 18)
9 fat quarters – Medium to dark prints/plaids	**Jacob's Ladder Blocks** Half-square triangles Four-Patch units **Virginia Reel Blocks** Rectangles Four-Patch on point	(1) 7¾" square per fabric (2) 2" strips per fabric (2) 3⅛" x 7⅝" rectangles per fabric (1) 6½" square per fabric (2) 5⅝" squares per fabric (2) 3⅛" squares per fabric	(HSTM – pg. 18) (FpP – pg. 19)
2 yds. – Very dark print or solid	**Borders**	(4) 4½" strips length of fabric	
1 yd. – Very dark print or solid	**Binding**	(8) 2¾" strips length of fabric	
4½ yds.	**Backing**	Seam the width or length of the quilt	
58" x 76"	**Batting**		

Each block is made from two different fabrics with 18 fabrics used in the quilt. There are two block designs. Each design will also have two blocks with the same two fabrics. Place the pieced blocks randomly for a scrappy look.

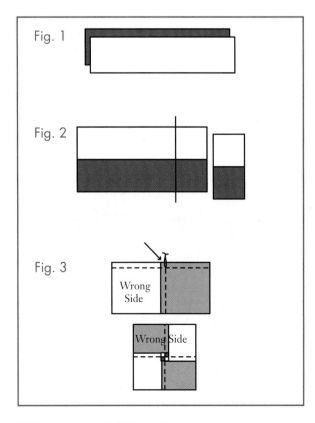

Fig. 1

Fig. 2

Fig. 3

Wrong Side

Wrong Side

Jacob's Ladder – Unit Assembly

HALF-SQUARE TRIANGLES: With right sides together, layer a 7¾" background square and a 7¾" medium square. Make 72 multiple pieced half-square triangles following the instructions on pg. 18. Each Jacob's Ladder block requires four half-square triangles.

FOUR-PATCH UNITS (Fig. 1): With right sides together, sew each 2" background strip together with a 2" medium strip. Open the strips, pressing the seam allowance toward the darker side.

(Fig. 2) Cut the sewn strips into 2" segments. Each Jacob's Ladder block requires ten segments. Sew two segments together, by turning one upside down. The seam allowances will abut each other. Make five Four-Patch units for each Jacob's Ladder block.

(Fig. 3) On the wrong side of each Four-Patch, unpick out the threads on both sides of the center, back to the crossing seam (arrow). Do not cut the threads. Press this center open.

The seam allowances will twirl around, making a center that will lay flat without lumpiness.

Jacob's Ladder – Block Assembly

Arrange the units in three rows, noting the alignment of the dark squares and triangles (see the Block Assembly diagram).

Press the seam allowances of the top and bottom row in one direction and the center row in the opposite direction so the seams abut each other when they are sewn together. Make 17 blocks.

Virginia Reel – Unit Assembly

Four-Patch on Point units (Fig. 4): Following the method on pg. 19, with right sides together, layer each 6½" background square together with a 6½" medium/dark square to make two quarter-square triangle units.

Continue on to make the Four-Patch on Point unit by attaching four, 3⅛" squares – two of background and two of medium/dark fabric – to opposite corners of the unit. Follow the instructions carefully and you'll have four bonus units you can save for another project. Press the seam allowances toward the square.

> NOTE: The orientation of the corners in the Four-Patch on Point units determines how the block spins. One block spins counterclockwise and the other has a clockwise spin. Make the blocks so they all spin in the same direction.

Virginia Reel – Block Assembly

Add four, 3⅛" x 7⅝" rectangles – two background and two medium to dark rectangles – to each Four-Patch on Point unit.

(Fig. 5) To begin, align the first rectangle with the right side of the unit as shown. Then, following the numbers, add rectangles around the unit. Finally, finish the seam between the first rectangle and the Four-Patch on Point unit.

At this point the block looks strange, but the next step will make it look the way it should.

(Fig. 6) Using 5⅜" background and medium/dark squares, add triangles to the corners of each block as you would in final step of making a square on point unit (pg. 19). Sew the squares to opposite corners with every addition. Watch the orientation of the blocks very carefully. Make 18 blocks.

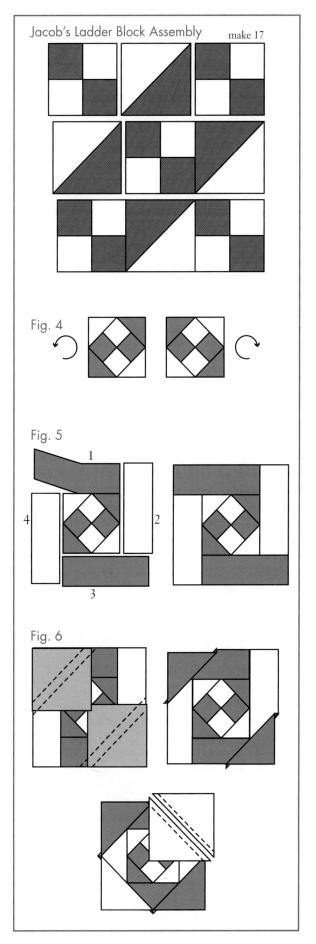

Jacob's Ladder Block Assembly   make 17

Fig. 4

Fig. 5

Fig. 6

Barbara Dieges

Virginia Reel Block · make 18

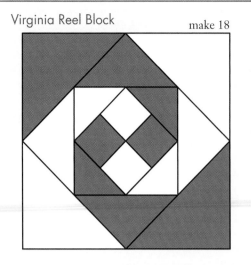

NOTE: There will be four bonus units left-over from making each Virginia Reel block to use for another project.

When rotated they make an interesting tessellated block (Fig. 8).

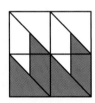
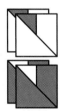

Fig. 9

Fig. 10

Quilt Assembly

Arrange the blocks in an alternating set (see the Block Assembly diagram). If the Virginia Reel blocks are spinning counterclockwise, arrange the Jacob's Ladder to look like Figure 9, otherwise rotate the Jacob's Ladder block to look like Figure 10.

Borders

Measure the height of the quilt top, including seam allowances. It should measure 63½". Trim two 4½" border strips to your measurement. Pin and sew to the sides.

Measure the width of the quilt top including the borders and seam allowances. It should measure 53½". Trim the remaining two strips to your measurement. Pin and sew to the top and bottom.

Quilting

This quilt is machine quilted diagonally through the small squares of the Jacob's Ladder blocks. A swirling design mimicking the spin of the Virginia Reel block is quilted continuously through those blocks.

Binding

The quilt has a finished ⅜" binding. See pg. 25 for binding techniques.

Quilt Assembly

Barbara Dieges

Books about our Quilting Heritage

America's Quilts and Coverlets, Carleton L. Safford and Robert S. Bishop. Bonanza Books, NY. 1985.

Aunt Jane of Kentucky, Eliza Hall Calvert. NCUP, Inc., Albany NY 1992.

Hearts and Hands–The Influence of Women & Quilts on American Society, Pat Ferrero, Elaine Hedges, and Julie Silber. Quilt Digest Press. San Francisco, CA. 1987.

Legacy–The Story of Talula Gilbert Bottoms and Her Quilts, Nancilu B. Burdick. Rutledge Hill Press, Nashville, TN. 1988.

North Carolina Quilts, edited by Ruth Haislip Roberson. The University of North Carolina Press. Chapel Hill, NC. 1988.

No Time on My Hands, Grace Snyder. University of Nebraska Press, NE. 1986.

Old Patchwork Quilts and the Women Who Made Them, Ruth E. Finley. EPM Publications, McLean, VA. 1992.

A Patchwork of Pieces–An Anthology of Early Quilt Stories, 1845–1940, compiled by Cuesta Ray Benberry and Carol Pinney Crabb. AQS, Paducah, KY. 1993.

Pieced from Ellen's Quilt–Ellen Spaulding Reed's Letters and Story, Linda Otto Lipsett. Quilt Digest Press. San Francisco, CA. 1991.

Pieces of the Past, Nancy Martin. That Patchwork Place, Bothell WA. 1986.

The Pieced Quilt–An American Design Tradition, Jonathan Holstein. A New York Graphic Society Book: Little, Brown and Company. Boston, MA. 1973.

Pioneer Women–Voices from the Kansas Frontier, Joanna L. Stratton. Simon and Schuster, NY. 1981.

Plain & Fancy–Country Quilts of the Pennsylvania-Germans, Anita Schorsch. Sterling Publishing Co., NY. 1992.

Plain and Fancy–Vermont's People and Their Quilts, as a Reflection of America, Richard L. Cleveland and Donna Bister. The Quilt Digest Press. Gualala, CA. 1991.

Quilts in America, Patsy and Myron Orlofsky. McGraw-Hill, NY. 1974

The Quilters, Women and Domestic Art: An Oral History, Patricia Cooper & Norma Bradley Allen. Doubleday, NY. 1989.

Quilts of the Oregon Trail–Treasures in the Trunk, Mary Bywater Cross. Rutledge Hill Press, Nashville, TN. 1993.

Remember Me, Women and their Friendship Quilts, Linda Otto Lipsett. Quilt Digest Press. San Francisco, CA. 1989.

The Romance of the Patchwork Quilt in America, Carrie A. Hall and Rose G. Kretsinger. The Caxton Printers Ltd., Caldwell, ID. 1935.

Small Endearments, 19th Century Quilts for Children and Dolls, Sandi Fox. Los Angeles Municipal Art Gallery Associates, LA. 1981.

Southern Quilts–Surviving Relics of the Civil War, Bets Ramsey and Merikay Waldvogel. Rutledge Hill Press. 1998.

Threads of Time, Nancy J. Martin. That Patchwork Place, Bothell, WA. 1990.

Treasures from Yesteryear, Books 1 and 2, Sharon Newman. That Patchwork Place, Bothell, WA. 1995.

To Love & To Cherish–Brides Remembered, Linda Otto Lipsett. Quilt Digest Press. San Francisco, CA. 1989.

The Unbroken Thread, Steve Hoare. Black Dome Press, Hensonville, NY. 1996.

Wrapped in Glory, Figurative Quilts and Bedcovers 1700–1900, Sandi Fox. Thames and Hudson, London. 1990.

Books about Quiltmaking

The American Quilt Story. The How-to and Heritage of a Craft Tradition, Susan Jenkins and Linda Seward. Rodale Press, Emmaus, PA. 1991.

Amish Quilting Patterns, Gwen Marston and Joe Cunningham. Dover Publications, Mineola NY. 1987.

Appliqué 12 Easy Ways, Elly Sienkiewicz. C & T Publishing, Lafayette, CA. 1991.

Encyclopiedia of Pieced Patterns, Compiled by Barbara Brackman. American Quilter's Society, Paducah, KY. 1993.

Fine Feathers–A Quilters Guide to Customizing Tradtional Feather Quilting Designs, Marianne Fons. C & T Publishing, Lafayette, CA. 1988.

Happy Endings–Finishing the Edges of Your Quilt, Mimi Dietrich. That Patchwork Place, Bothell, WA. 1987.

Heirloom Machine Quilting, Harriet Hargrave. C & T Publishing, Lafayette, CA. 1995.

The Ins and Outs: Perfecting the Quilting Stitch, Patricia J. Morris. American Quilter's Society, Paducah, KY. 2001.

Mastering Quilt Marking, Pepper Cory. C & T Publishing, Lafayette, CA. 1999.

The Quilter's Album of Blocks and Borders, Jinny Beyer. EPM Publications, McLean, VA. 1980.

The Quilt Design Workbook, Beth and Jeffrey Gutcheon. Rawson Associates Publishers, Inc. 1976.

Quilting Designs from the Amish, Pepper Cory. Culpepper's Press, East Lansing, MI. 1985.

Quilting Design Sourcebook, Dorothy Osler. That Patchwork Place, Bothell, WA. 1996.

Quilts from a Different Angle, Sara Nephew. That Patchwork Place, Bothell, WA. 1986.

Quilts! Quilts! Quilts! The Complete Guide to Quiltmaking, Diana McClun and Laura Nownes. The Quilt Digest Press, Gualala, CA. 1998.

Rotary Magic, Nancy Johnson-Srebro. Rodale Press, Emmaus, PA. 1998.

Stars and Flowers, Three Sided Patchwork, Sara Nephew. That Patchwork Place, Bothell, WA. 1989.

A Treasury of Quilting Designs, Linda Goodmon Emery. American Quilter's Society, Paducah, KY. 1990.

Trip Around the World Quilts–A New Approach, Blanche Yound and Helen Young. Young Publications, Oakview, CA. 1980.

RESOURCES
The author's preferences include the following brand name items:

Sewing Machine Needles
Schmetz™ Jeans/Denim 80/12 or
Schmetz™ Quilting 75/11 – 90/12

Handwork Needles
Clover™ Gold Eye #12 Betweens – quilting
Clover™ #12 Betweens or Sharps – appliqué

Thread
Mettler™ Silk finish 100% cotton thread, size 50 – hand appliqué, machine piecing, and machine quilting
Mettler™ 100% cotton quilting thread, size 40 – hand quilting

Rulers
Omnigrid™ rulers
Quilter's Quarter™

Markers
Quilter's Quarter Marker™
Quilter's Pencil™ – mechanical pencil
Roxanne's™ white and silver pencils

Thimbles and Finger Protectors
Roxanne's™ thimble
Aunt Becky's™ Finger Protector

ABOUT the AUTHOR

Since early childhood, Barbara Dieges has been working with threads and fabrics. Her grandmother and aunts always found ways to keep her little hands busy with needlework.

After graduating from college, Barbara taught kindergarten before starting her family. While raising three children, she designed for Bucilla Yarn and developed her own line of stitchery kits. She taught creative stitchery, cross-stitch, and needlepoint at local needlework shops and various parks and recreation centers.

Barbara made her first quilt in 1969 for her first child, but it was in 1982 that she became a dedicated quilter. She has had several years of in-depth study of quilt history, design, and techniques with both traditional and non-traditional quilt teachers.

As a member of two quilt guilds, she is involved in all phases of quilting. Her quilts are consistent award winners and have been exhibited nationally. Even though she travels to teach and lecture nationally, she still takes time to share her expertise with local shops and her guilds.

For more information about Barbara, visit her website, *bdieges.com*

This is only a small selection of the books available from the American Quilter's Society. AQS books are known worldwide for timely topics, clear writing, beautiful color photos, and accurate illustrations and patterns. The following books are available from your local bookseller, quilt shop, or public library.

#6073   us$19.95

#4957   us$34.95

#4827   us$24.95

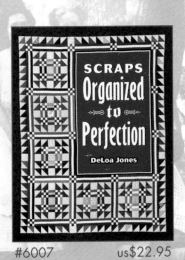

#6007   us$22.95

#5763   us$21.95

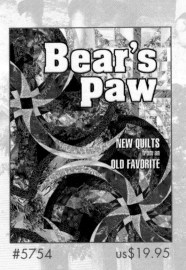

#5754   us$19.95

#6036   us$24.95

#5756   us$19.95

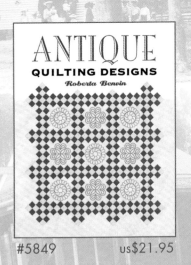

#5849   us$21.95

Look for these books nationally or call **1-800-626-5420**